Everyday Chef

Everyday Chef

Simple Recipes for Family and Friends

Jeremy Sewall & Erin Byers Murray

PHOTOGRAPHY BY **Michael Harlan Turkell**

RIZZOLI
NEW YORK

New York Paris London Milan

Contents

Contents

Introduction

I've been a professional chef for nearly thirty years. But truth be told, my wife, Lisa, has historically done most of the cooking at home. She's also a trained chef and we met in a kitchen (of course) when she was a pastry chef. For her, cooking has never been the hard part. The hard part is appealing to children of various ages while making meals that adults will enjoy as well. And even as our kids have gotten older—and as I've jumped in to share more of the home-cooking responsibilities—the challenges remain. She's busy, the kids' palates are all different, and it takes time. Cooking at home for a family can be just as complex as cooking at a restaurant for guests.

When writing recipes, my goal has always been to present the techniques and ingredients I use in restaurant kitchens in a way that cooks can easily apply at home. And while it's fun to write about what I've done in professional kitchens and to imagine people creating those dishes in their own kitchens, the reality is that that's not how most people cook and eat most days. I approach food differently at home; the rules are relaxed and the goals are a little different. I still sometimes have to cook for picky eaters but, ultimately, the goal is to share a meal together.

If you pressed me to find a silver lining in the Covid pandemic, it was that it gave me time to cook for my family at home. It already seems like a lifetime ago, but as the world was learning to make sourdough starters and flour disappeared from grocery store shelves, I, too, got busy in the kitchen. Not that I hadn't cooked at home before that, but I didn't usually prepare two to three meals a day. I was in charge of holiday meals and the occasional dinner, especially when guests came over. I did lots of grilling during the summer; Sundays during football season were my shining moment. (I love game-day food, especially the tacos for a crowd you can read about on page 210.)

So, when all five of us were home for months on end, cooking became a great distraction and a way to fill up the day. It also filled the void left when my restaurants closed. If all you've done for nearly thirty years is run restaurants, stopping cold stings. I am so glad restaurants are back open and love them now more than I ever did—but I'm also grateful that the downtime gave me opportunities to cook in ways I hadn't before. Cooking at home helped me remember why I fell in love with food to begin with.

Both my parents were born and raised in southern Maine. My dad had a job that required us to move around—he was an engineer who worked in large manufacturing plants for Georgia Pacific. My older sisters were born in Maine and my little sister and I were born in Illinois. After my first few years of life, we moved to Ohio, which is where I developed an interest in food. We lived on a long road with just six houses on it, and in between the houses was a working farm with horses, cows, goats, and other animals. The fields were planted with alfalfa, soy, and corn. We ended up with a family pet from the neighbor's farm: Mitsy, a barn cat who was just as mean on her last day as she was on her first. (She made everyone in the family bleed at least once.) We also got a couple of pet rabbits from the farm. The farm raised them for fur, but ours were spared for my four sisters to have as pets. (I always wanted to see one skinned, but I was in the first grade so I wasn't allowed to observe the process for fear it would traumatize me.)

I remember drinking warm goat's milk from the neighbor's farm. It took a little convincing to get me to try it. But I loved it. I expected it to be cold but the warm, super-rich milk was better than anything that came out of our fridge. There was also a big cherry tree in our backyard, and I remember my hands being stained from eating cherries off the tree. (Spitting the pits at my sisters was a favorite pastime.) I loved the raw fruit from the tree more than my mom's cooked pie filling, and I found it so cool that something grew on a tree and I could eat it. We also had a garden and my parents canned the harvest as any sensible Yankee couple would. My mother made the best dill pickles I've ever had, even to this day.

In the summer of 1979, we moved to the Hudson Valley in New York. All the same basic food values came along: we had another big garden and continued to can our own food. We were surrounded by orchards, and the other neighborhood kids and I would sneak in to grab a few apples. I grew up eating mostly home-cooked meals—protein, starch, and vegetables were almost always on the menu. We usually had a hot breakfast of oatmeal, waffles, French toast, pancakes, or eggs on the weekends, and I brought a homemade lunch to school with me until I was a senior in high school. My sisters were always making desserts.

During this time, I learned about the local butcher, Wade's Meats, where my mom got flank steak, lamb burgers wrapped in bacon, and other inexpensive cuts that could feed a family of seven. I loved going to Wade's in the fall because all the local hunters would drop off their deer to be butchered. The carcasses hung inside and outside of the shop—I was both shocked and excited to see them all lined up, waiting their turn. Hunters got back the prime cuts and lots of tasty sausage—but some years, there were so many deer, I wondered if they really gave the right one back to the hunter who had brought it in.

Meanwhile, there were pick-your-own berry patches and roadside corn stands that put out a coffee can where you could leave your money. All of it became part of our regular meal planning at the house. Food was an event and family dinner was exactly that: a time to enjoy simple food and talk about our days.

Mixed into all of this were annual trips to southern Maine, about a four-hour drive, where most of the rest of our family still lived. These trips became the highlight of my year. My grandfather had been a lobsterman since the 1940s, and to this day my cousin Mark catches lobster for my restaurants. Fishing trips brought in mackerel, cod, pollock, and flounder—all treats for us visitors. At a young age, I came to love catching fish (often far more than eating it; thankfully that's changed). At least once a summer, we'd have a lobster cookout, and we usually brought a few extra cooked lobsters home to New York.

My grandparents, aunts, and uncles all had large gardens that seemed much better kept than ours, with a large variety of crops. Between picking berries and digging potatoes, I would keep busy gathering food. I remember these details, yet I can't tell you what types of presents I got for birthdays, Christmas, or my first communion. My love of food started through the lens of a boy who loved the process: catching, picking, digging, and eating.

When we were a little older, my sisters waitressed at a very small airport cafe near our house that was only open on the weekends. Eventually, my dad bought the cafe and ran it himself. It was a small place where you were likely to know the person eating next to you. The regulars were all hobby flyers who took out their own planes on the weekends. My sisters were the cooks and servers and they made soups and desserts; I washed dishes on weekends when I wasn't playing baseball or fishing. There was always a line for breakfast when we prepared homemade waffles with berries. At the cafe I learned to make French fries, fry an egg, read tickets, and wash dishes, all of which came in handy when I realized I wanted to become a chef.

Now that I identify as a chef, I see how all of those past experiences set me up to appreciate the ingredients I reach for. I've been fortunate to have had a career that allows me to work with the best: truffles, caviar, lobster, wild mushrooms. At one point, they were like trophies on the menu, items I wanted to showcase. The sources for these ingredients have always been sacred—sometimes chefs share these secrets with one another, but often we don't. Over the years, I've seen trends and ingredients rise and fall in popularity—right now, we're at a moment when vegetables are front and center and chefs are excited about working with previously lesser-used cuts of meat and fish.

We're also at a point when we can see what is out there more clearly than ever, thanks to social media and the internet. Good food is everywhere, and so is inspiration. This brings me back to cooking at home. Cooking at home has taken on new meaning for me. Often I find that it takes me back to my early days, to enjoying the simple pleasure of eating dinner together at my family's table, and those years I spent as a young chef, discovering new ideas, finding inspiration everywhere. Now, I have the experience of a lifelong career and find that the basic skills I learned early on in restaurant kitchens directly apply to the home kitchen, too: time management, organization, planning, and, ultimately, execution.

That all brings us to why I'm writing this cookbook. Whether you are planning a big meal for a gathering of family or friends, or simply a quick bite for an early dinner or weekend brunch, every meal offers the opportunity to nourish and to provide a memory. (I'll never forget my mother's lumpy, overcooked mashed potatoes. We always complained about them but we couldn't imagine Thanksgiving without them.) Home-cooked meals can be a way to connect and share a moment. Now, with my kids grown, anytime we all get to sit down to eat together is a truly special event.

My goal with *Everyday Chef* is to encourage you to create your own experiences and memories with a home-cooked meal. Whether it's grilling outside with friends on a summer day, eating perfect tomatoes, corn on the cob, and beautifully grilled steaks, or making pancakes with your kids, find the meals that you enjoy making and do it often. Don't be afraid of mistakes. The point is to enjoy the process, take time to plan things out, and look for great ingredients. From that starting point, it's easy to share a meal—and make a memory—with the people you love and enjoy most.

Notes for a Home Cook

Get Comfortable in the Kitchen

Whether you're new to cooking or have been doing it daily for years, set yourself up for success. Mentally, that means planning ahead, knowing who you're cooking for, and reminding yourself to stay nimble. From a resource standpoint, it means stocking your pantry with the right ingredients, having a few key pieces of equipment on hand, and shopping strategically. Once you've got those elements in place, shopping for, preparing, and cooking meals at home should be easy—and fun.

Plan Your Meals

Time management is important—you want to enjoy a meal with the people you're cooking it for and being organized on the front end will get you there. Do your shopping a day ahead and prep what you can in advance. Having garlic peeled and vegetables chopped will set you up for fewer stressful moments as you reach the final stretch of putting the meal together.

Know Your Audience

Anytime I have guests over, I like to ask a couple of quick questions first: their likes and dislikes, any allergies or preferences. It might feel odd at the time, but there is nothing worse than making clam pasta for someone who has a shellfish allergy. While I always encourage people to try new things, being in-the-know on people's preferences will make it easier for everyone to enjoy the meal.

. . . Especially When It Comes to Kids

A truth most new parents have a hard time learning: Kids should eat what you make them—but they won't. Having raised three kids, each with their own likes and aversions, even as a chef I can tell you that no parent has it easy when it comes to feeding children. And nothing ruins a meal quicker than a child refusing to eat.

My tip is not to push them too hard. Constantly introduce new foods and if they don't like something or won't try it, wait it out and attempt it again. Over time, all kids develop a taste for new things. Believe me, it's better to make simple adjustments to the recipe you're already planning to cook than to have them eat a bowl of cereal for dinner. Use a few simple tricks instead, like setting aside some plain pasta before adding it to the intended dish or preparing meat that they can identify before adding it to the final dish. And as often as you can, get them involved. Teach them how to pull the husks off corn or fold a dumpling—if they're involved, they're more likely to eat the food. Make them part of the process as best you can.

Don't Forget to Sit Down and Eat

I like to serve meals family-style, putting everything on the table and letting people help themselves. Passing dishes to one another is a ceremony of sorts. Everyone should sit together and enjoy the meal. During Covid, for my family and so many others, there was a real return to the dinner table. Rather than once or twice a week when we all happened to be home, eating together became a nightly experience. In today's busy world, it's hard to make that happen as much as we would like, but try to do it every chance you get. It's important. Food is communal and the conversations that come with each meal are priceless.

Start Simple and Stay Nimble

If you are new to cooking, start simple. Some of the humblest meals can be the best. Build on your successes and learn from your failures; both are bound to happen. By staying nimble I mean don't be afraid to substitute ingredients with what you have on hand. And don't worry if things start to get off track. It's just food! The most important thing is to enjoy the process and keep trying.

The Importance of Great Ingredients

As a chef, I've been on a quest for the best and most unique ingredients for most of my career. I hope it's a journey that never ends. The feeling of having that perfect ingredient in your hand is almost as rewarding as plating the final dish. Home cooks should reach for that same high standard. When you learn about different vegetable varieties, understand seasonality, and finally find that one excellent olive oil, you're taking steps to developing your cooking and setting yourself up to produce a lifetime of great meals.

Great ingredients don't have to be expensive or hard-to-find. Some of the best meals come from the humblest of ingredients. That said, be picky. Whatever you acquire should look and feel fresh and be visibly absent of bruises, nicks, brown edges, or soft spots. Meats should have good color and look freshly cut, without any foreign odors or colors. Fish should be bright and odorless; it should not be sitting in liquid or piled awkwardly. Inexpensive cuts of meat and poultry should hit the same standard as anything else you're buying. And always look for the busy meat and seafood counters—finding the right meat counter, butcher, or fishmonger will make all the difference in your shopping and cooking experience.

One of the best things about cooking today is that most ingredients are just a few clicks away. Access to specialty ingredients is easier than ever since they can be delivered to your doorstep—it's a remarkable time to be an ambitious home cook. But if you miss the days of feeling like you were on a scavenger hunt for one little-known ingredient, head to your nearest specialty or international grocery store. Not only will you be supporting a small local business, but walking the aisles could lead to the discovery of your next new ingredient and another cooking adventure.

Buy What You Need and Save Your Leftovers

Try not to buy more than you are going to use. And when purchasing ingredients that come in large quantities, try to find multiple uses for those ingredients.

Besides the leftovers that you might have from a cooked dish, some recipes leave you with little bits and pieces of ingredients. This is where a good home cook can learn to be flexible and versatile. Food waste is a big problem, so let's not add to it: Try to find a use for everything. This is a great opportunity to try new recipes and develop a few of your own.

If you have leftover vegetables after chopping what you need for a specific recipe, find other uses for them. I like adding extra bits and ends to a rice bowl or cooking them into a frittata. Most basic vegetables, like onions, carrots, celery, and mushroom stems, can be used to make a flavorful vegetable stock. You can freeze them individually after making a recipe and pull all of them out when you're ready to make a stock.

Extra pieces of raw meat and poultry can be frozen and saved for a stir-fry or a rice bowl, or be thrown into a food processor for meatballs or a custom burger. Leftovers from a meal are also great to share. I keep a couple of extra glass containers with lids handy to send home with friends after a big meal.

Farmer's Markets and CSAs

Seasonal markets and farmstands are my favorite places to shop. Freshly harvested produce piled high, with a little dirt around the edges, gets ideas flowing. Markets can be overwhelming, especially when produce is at its peak. Start small and simple: buy ingredients you're familiar with or go in with a plan. If the seller doesn't have what you're looking for, ask what they do have and what they might do with it. When you get your bounty home, use it as soon as you can—produce is at its peak when it gets to the market and shouldn't sit around. If you're part of a CSA (community-supported agriculture) program, even better. A CSA delivers a box of items on a predetermined schedule. Joining a CSA is a great way to experiment with new varieties of produce, since the delivery is usually a mix of seasonal items that the farmer is proud to harvest. Using them may require research and planning, but if you lean into it, you're bound to discover some new recipes and dishes to share.

A Well-Stocked Pantry

Salt and Pepper

Most often when I call for salt and pepper in this cookbook, I mean kosher salt and freshly ground black pepper. My go-to kosher salt is Diamond Crystal—I've used it for most of my career and know how it feels in my hand when I season food. Sometimes I specify sea salt or another type of pepper, such as white pepper. When I use big flakes of sea salt to finish a dish, it's generally the last thing I add just before serving.

Oils

I generally cook in canola oil, as it's good for frying, sautéing, or brushing on meats before grilling. It has a neutral flavor and works for marinades and dressings as well as high-heat cooking. Grapeseed oil is a great alternative for cooking but more expensive.

Some olive oils can be used for cooking, but mostly they are better for finishing dishes or using in marinades and vinaigrettes. Always seek out extra-virgin olive oil. There are many varieties and labels of olive oil from all over the world; some of my favorites come from Spain, Greece, and California. Research and taste a few olive oils side by side to determine your favorite. Once you find a good one, stick with it.

I call for toasted sesame oil a few times in this book. It has a strong flavor that adds another dimension.

Vinegars and Other Acids

Good vinegar is just as important as good olive oil. The basic vinegars I like to have on hand are sherry, cider, rice wine, balsamic, and champagne. Each has a specific flavor and, when used correctly, can really brighten a dish. Besides being a key ingredient in pickling, vinegar can be used to season a sauce or drizzle over meat, fish, and vegetables. Incorporating acid in the form of freshly squeezed lemon juice is my number one way to add flavor to a dish—you'll see I use it frequently. I like to keep lemons, limes, and oranges on hand at all times.

Fresh Herbs

Nearly all of my recipes call for fresh herbs. If you want to substitute dry herbs, please do—don't let anything be a speed bump that stops you from making dinner. Store fresh herbs in the fridge wrapped in a paper towel or a kitchen cloth; if you're not using them within a day or two, use a damp paper towel.

Pasta

I love making and eating fresh egg pasta, but kneading the dough, rolling it out into sheets, and cutting it into noodles doesn't easily fit into a family dinner plan. You can buy fresh pasta at the grocery store or a specialty store. Just be sure to use store-bought fresh pasta shortly after you get it home. Dried pasta has a long shelf life and is a great ingredient to stock in your pantry. There are endless varieties of dried pasta available at most grocery stores. Be sure to examine the ingredient label—the fewer ingredients the better. Brand-name pastas are great for every-night cooking, but I like to look for artisan dried pasta, which will be pale in color and might even have a rough texture to it. If you have eaten generic dried pasta your whole life, you might be surprised by the quality of artisan dried pasta. Try different shapes and sizes and be sure to read the package instructions for the correct cooking time. If you're finishing the pasta by adding it to a sauce, cook it for 1 to 2 minutes less than what the instructions call for, so that it can finish cooking in the final steps of the recipe.

Legumes

Chickpeas and beans can be an inexpensive main protein component or addition to a meal. There's nothing wrong with canned beans—and they're great when you're pressed for time—but cooking dried legumes yields delicious results and is a skill worth learning. (See page 229 for instructions.) Always store dried legumes in a sealed container in your pantry.

Grains

My go-to grains are rice, quinoa (not technically a grain, but treated like one), and barley. They take on flavors well and are versatile. Store these in sealed containers in your pantry.

Staples

Keep the following condiments stocked and you will always be able to create a good meal:

Aleppo pepper

Chili flakes

Dijon mustard

Grainy mustard

Honey

Hot sauce (good old Tabasco and sriracha are my go-tos)

Maple syrup

Pickles (I always have dill and bread-and-butter in my fridge)

Sambal chili paste

Soy sauce

Your favorite mayonnaise (There are plenty of recipes out there, including in my other books, for making your own mayonnaise. For the purposes of this cookbook, I suggest buying a jar of your favorite mayonnaise and dressing it up as directed.)

Stocks

Good stocks are important in cooking. In these recipes I call for the basics: chicken and vegetable stock. Many of the recipes here start with a plain stock that is then fortified. I didn't include stock recipes in this cookbook, but they are easy to find. If you make your own stock, freeze it in small batches that will be ready to defrost when needed. You can also buy high-quality stock. Look for low-sodium choices, as stocks are often reduced, which can give overly salty results. You can always add more salt, but you can't take it out.

Equipment and Gear

You could spend a small fortune filling your kitchen with gadgets and pans. I recommend sticking with a few basics to start—you can always add new equipment as you add new recipes.

Pots and Pans

Buy a few good stainless-steel sauce and sauté pans; a heavy-bottomed pan that holds heat and has a sturdy handle; a large, tall pot for cooking pasta and blanching vegetables; and a couple of good nonstick sauté pans, especially for beginners. (They make sautéing fish and cooking eggs a lot easier.)

Baking Sheets

I use half- and quarter-sheet pans for everything from seasoning and holding food items to baking. They are true kitchen workhorses.

Wire Racks

Based on your assortment of sheet pans, it's good to have wire racks that fit into them. When roasting meat, bacon, or large vegetables, place those items on a wire rack set over a baking sheet to allow the heat to be distributed evenly around whatever you are cooking. This ensures that it will be evenly cooked through. I also like to have a poultry rack on hand for roasting chicken.

Knives and Cutting Boards

Knives should be sharp and ready to use. I recommend a basic French knife, a thin slicing knife, a flexible boning knife, and a serrated paring knife. The latter is my go-to, since it stays sharp with little effort. You'll also need one or two good cutting boards. I like to have at least one large wooden cutting board for carving up larger pieces of meat or poultry, as well as a few smaller plastic ones that are easier to move and clean.

Appliances

Invest in a basic food processor and a blender. A rice cooker and a slow cooker are also very handy, and while it's not a necessity, frying in a countertop fryer is much easier than frying in a pan of hot oil and gives you greater control.

Storage

Gather a selection of glass containers with lids, which are good for storing leftovers. (I opt for glass over plastic because the glass doesn't pick up odors and flavors like plastic does; it's also better for the environment.) I also recommend getting a set of stackable glass bowls to help organize ingredients. You will be amazed how often you use them—and how much they'll help you keep your recipes on track.

Chapter 1
Breakfast

When my kids were young, I had it in my head that since I worked nights in the restaurant business and missed a lot of dinners at home, I should be sure to get up and have breakfast with them before we all started our days. It was a great idea in theory, but I failed to make it to the table more times than I'd like to admit. When it did happen, it was always a great start to the day. As a family, we still love gathering over breakfast when we're all back together—but these days, it tends to happen later since we all like to sleep in. These recipes are for those who like to eat early, as well as those who like to make that first meal more of a brunch or lunch.

Breakfast can be a great time to get creative, since recipes for the first meal of the day tend to be simple. My tip for breakfast is to do your prep work the night before so you can sip coffee and not worry about messing up too badly before you're fully awake. Get any knife work out of the way and measure your dry and wet ingredients in advance so you can get up and just assemble in the morning.

Find the recipes you love and make them again and again. My kids are grown and I miss those days. But when they do come home, they always request their childhood favorites.

One more tip: Don't be afraid to have breakfast for dinner once in a while.

Poached Eggs with Smoked Salmon and Salsa Verde   SERVES 4

LET'S BE HONEST: poached eggs and smoked salmon aren't going to be a weekday go-to. Instead, this is a dish we pull out when we're having friends over for brunch. But you can easily take elements of this—like the toast, avocado, and salsa verde—and make them into a quick and easy breakfast. There are many good brands of smoked salmon out there, but I like to make it at home—it's not that hard to do. (I lay out easy instructions in *The Row 34 Cookbook*.) I also love the versatility of salsa verde, which really shines alongside eggs and fish. Find a crusty sourdough to accompany this dish—and make sure the avocado is ripe.

1 ripe avocado

4 slices sourdough bread, toasted

Kosher salt and freshly ground black pepper

8 ounces sliced smoked salmon

4 Poached Eggs (page 228)

¾ cup Salsa Verde (recipe follows)

Cut the avocado in half lengthwise and remove the pit. Use a large spoon to scoop the flesh from each half and place on a cutting board, cut-side down. Thinly slice each half. Arrange a few slices of avocado on each piece of toast and season with salt and pepper. Top the avocado with a few slices of smoked salmon. Carefully place a poached egg on top of each piece of toast and spoon 1 to 2 tablespoons of salsa verde over the top. Serve the remaining salsa verde on the side.

Salsa Verde   MAKES ¾ CUP

Place all of the ingredients in a food processor and pulse until well combined.

2 cups flat-leaf parsley leaves

½ cup extra-virgin olive oil

1 clove garlic, peeled

Zest and juice of 1 lemon

2 teaspoons capers, rinsed

2 teaspoons Dijon mustard

¼ teaspoon chili flakes

2 anchovy fillets (optional)

Kosher salt and freshly ground black pepper

Chef's Tip: The best way to cut an avocado is to place it on a cutting board, split it in half lengthwise, remove the pit, then use a large spoon to scoop the flesh away from the skin using one smooth scoop. The avocado flesh can then be evenly sliced or cubed.

Scrambled Eggs with Mushrooms and Shallots SERVES 4

8 large eggs

½ cup half-and-half

2 tablespoons canola oil

1 cup sliced cremini
    mushrooms

2 tablespoons unsalted butter

2 large shallots, thinly sliced

2 tablespoons crème fraîche or
    sour cream

Kosher salt and freshly ground
    black pepper

4 slices sourdough bread,
    toasted

1 teaspoon fresh thyme leaves

Chef's Tip: Incorporating crème fraîche into eggs while scrambling results in a fluffier texture and a richer flavor.

THERE ARE AS MANY WAYS to scramble eggs as there are people who make them, but I really love buttery scrambled eggs. I use cremini mushrooms, but feel free to get creative—wild mushrooms, like morels or chanterelles, bring this recipe to the next level. Just make sure the mushrooms are washed well. Using a good nonstick sauté pan and a flexible rubber spatula will make this dish super easy to execute.

Crack the eggs into a mixing bowl and whisk in the half-and-half; strain through a fine-mesh strainer and let sit at room temperature.

Heat the canola oil in a nonstick sauté pan over medium-high heat. Add the mushrooms and cook until they begin to brown lightly.

Reduce the heat to medium and add the butter and shallots. Cook until the shallots are softened and start to brown lightly. Add the eggs and stir constantly, moving them around the pan with a rubber spatula. When they begin to firm up, add the crème fraîche and season with salt and pepper. Continue stirring until the mixture is cooked through but not stiff. Remove from the heat. Spoon the egg mixture on top of the toasted sourdough slices. Top with additional black pepper and thyme leaves before serving.

Baked Eggs with Spiced Potatoes SERVES 4

I LOVE COOKING in cast-iron skillets—some dishes just call for a heavy, heat-retaining tool. If you add cast-iron cookware to your collection, take the time to season it well and use it often to give it that beautiful sheen. These skillets will literally last you a lifetime—my grandmother's pans must be close to eighty years old and still work perfectly. They're just right for this baked egg dish, which you can make for breakfast, brunch, or even lunch. I use ham here—be sure to use a ham steak, not deli ham—but you can also substitute bacon or breakfast sausage. Look for golf ball–size red potatoes and leave the skins on. If you don't have a cast-iron skillet, just sauté everything together and transfer to a baking dish, then add the eggs right before it goes into the oven.

Preheat the oven to 350°F.

On a baking sheet, toss the potato wedges with the olive oil, smoked paprika, and turmeric and season with salt and pepper. Bake for 15 minutes, then remove and allow to cool. (The potatoes will be just barely cooked.) Leave the oven on.

Cut off the ends of the broccoli rabe, remove the large leaves, and slice the stalks and tops into ½-inch pieces.

In a 10-inch cast-iron skillet, heat the canola oil over medium heat. Add the onion and sauté until it begins to color, 3 to 4 minutes. Add the ham and cook until it just starts to brown, about 2 minutes. Add the broccoli rabe and garlic and sauté, stirring frequently, until everything begins to soften, 3 to 4 minutes.

Remove the pan from the heat and stir in the potatoes, chopped tomato and reserved juices, and the stock; season with salt and pepper. Place the skillet over medium heat and bring to a gentle simmer. Remove from the heat and, with the back of a measuring scoop, make 4 small wells for the eggs to sit in. Crack 1 egg into each well. Carefully transfer the pan to the oven and bake for 12 minutes. Serve with toast, if using.

5 red potatoes, washed and cut into wedges

2 tablespoons extra-virgin olive oil

½ teaspoon smoked paprika

¼ teaspoon turmeric

Kosher salt and freshly ground black pepper

1 bunch broccoli rabe

3 tablespoons canola oil

1 small Spanish onion, thinly sliced

1 pound ham steak, skin trimmed off and steak diced

2 cloves garlic, chopped

1 beefsteak tomato, cored and diced, juices reserved

¼ cup chicken or vegetable stock

4 large eggs

4 slices crusty bread, toasted (optional)

Spinach and Goat Cheese Frittata SERVES 4

8 large eggs

½ cup half-and-half

¼ cup sour cream

Kosher salt and freshly ground
    black pepper

2 tablespoons extra-virgin
    olive oil

1 large shallot, thinly sliced

2 cups baby spinach leaves

½ cup crumbled firm goat
    cheese

3 cups baby greens

2 small breakfast radishes,
    thinly sliced

3 tablespoons Champagne
    Vinaigrette (page 75)

½ teaspoon Aleppo pepper
    (optional)

MY SISTER JENNIFER says she loves to make frittatas because you can put almost anything in them and they will taste good. She's right. This baked egg dish has a million possibilities, and this simple version is the ideal place to start. A nonstick skillet is your best friend for this recipe—I strongly encourage nonstick for anyone who is new to cooking eggs. If you'd rather not use goat cheese, you could try gouda or Gruyère here. Adding a simple salad on top turns this into a complete meal.

Preheat the oven to 350ºF.

In a large bowl, whisk together the eggs, half-and-half, and sour cream, and season with salt and pepper.

Place a 10-inch nonstick, oven-safe sauté pan over medium heat and add the olive oil. Once the oil is shimmering, add the shallot and cook until it begins to color lightly. Add the spinach and stir gently with a rubber spatula, moving the pan over the heat as the spinach wilts. Once the spinach has wilted, pour the egg mixture into the pan. Use the spatula to mix everything well, pulling the eggs in from the edge of the pan toward the center as they cook and allowing the uncooked egg to run out to the edge. Once the eggs are set on the bottom, remove the pan from the heat. Sprinkle the crumbled goat cheese over top. Transfer the pan to the oven and bake for 12 minutes.

While the frittata is in the oven, in a bowl toss the baby greens with the sliced radishes and vinaigrette.

Carefully remove the pan from the oven and allow to cool for a few minutes. Holding the pan at an angle, use a clean spatula to slide the frittata onto a serving plate. Cut into 4 wedges and top with the salad. Garnish with Aleppo pepper, if using.

Brioche French Toast with Brown Butter Bananas SERVES 4

THIS DISH IS just as good for dessert as it is for breakfast—and your kitchen will smell incredible as the toasty cinnamon mixes with the aroma of buttery brioche. You can assemble the batter and slice the brioche the night before to save yourself a little time. I also sometimes toast the bread in advance and reheat the slices in the oven right before serving. Be sure to whisk the egg mixture well just before soaking the bread to distribute the cinnamon evenly, and then slice and add bananas at the last minute so they keep their color and texture.

Preheat the oven to 350°F.

In a large bowl, whisk the cinnamon with 3 tablespoons water until completely dissolved to make a thin paste. Whisk in the eggs, milk, and vanilla.

In a large sauté pan or on a large griddle, heat 1 tablespoon of the canola oil over medium-high heat. Add 2 slices of brioche to the bowl of batter and allow to soak, turning to coat both sides. Transfer the slices to the pan or griddle and toast for 2 to 3 minutes on each side until lightly browned. Move toasted bread to a baking sheet in a single layer and repeat with remaining slices, adding 1 tablespoon oil to the pan before toasting each batch. Once finished, place the baking sheet in the oven for 6 minutes to warm the slices.

Meanwhile, in a medium saucepan, melt the butter over medium heat until it begins to brown lightly. Whisk in the brown sugar and simmer for 2 minutes. Whisk in the heavy cream and raise the heat to bring the mixture to a boil. Remove from the heat and fold in the banana slices. Season with the salt.

To serve, place two French toast slices on each plate and top with the brown butter bananas.

1 tablespoon ground cinnamon

3 large eggs, beaten

¼ cup whole milk

2 teaspoons vanilla extract

¼ cup canola oil

8 slices brioche, about 2 inches thick

1 stick (8 tablespoons) unsalted butter

¼ cup brown sugar

¼ cup heavy cream

4 bananas, sliced

Pinch kosher salt

Chef's Tip: Leave the sliced brioche uncovered on the counter for a few hours or overnight to let it dry out a bit, which will help it absorb the batter.

Whole Wheat Pancakes with Warm Berries and Whipped Mascarpone **SERVES 4**

PANCAKES

2 large eggs

2 cups buttermilk

3 tablespoons unsalted butter, melted, plus more for the griddle

2 teaspoons kosher salt

1 teaspoon ground cinnamon

2 teaspoons baking powder

1 teaspoon baking soda

1 cup all-purpose flour

1½ cups whole wheat flour

BERRIES

½ cup granulated sugar

1 cup sliced strawberries

¼ cup blueberries

¼ cup raspberries

½ cup blackberries

2 tablespoons cornstarch

MASCARPONE

1 cup mascarpone, at room temperature

1 teaspoon salt

¼ cup honey

WHEN MY KIDS WERE LITTLE, pancakes offered them an opportunity to ingest as much maple syrup as possible. Naturally, they resisted when I introduced berries to our pancake routine, as the fruit got in the way of their syrup intake. Nowadays, they actually go for the fruit. Whole wheat flour has more nutrients than white flour and delivers more robust flavor. These pancakes aren't too sweet, especially with the tang of the buttermilk.

For the pancakes, in a medium bowl, whisk the eggs, buttermilk, and the 3 tablespoons melted butter. In a larger bowl, mix together the salt, cinnamon, baking powder, baking soda, and flours. Transfer the wet ingredients to the dry ingredients and whisk vigorously until there are no longer any lumps. Let the batter rest for 10 minutes.

Meanwhile, for the berries, in a saucepan combine ¼ cup water with the sugar. Place over medium heat and stir until the sugar is dissolved. Add half of each type of berry and slowly bring to a boil over medium-high heat. Reduce the heat to medium-low and simmer for 8 minutes. In a small bowl, whisk together ¼ cup tepid water and the cornstarch, then whisk the mixture into the saucepan to combine with the berries. Simmer for 2 additional minutes. Remove the pan from the heat and use an immersion blender to puree the berries until smooth. Strain the mixture through a fine-mesh strainer into a heatproof bowl and return to the saucepan; fold in the remaining whole berries. Keep warm.

For the mascarpone, in a stand mixer fitted with the paddle attachment, whip together the mascarpone, honey, and salt on medium speed until light and airy.

Place a nonstick griddle over medium heat and melt about 1 tablespoon butter. When the butter starts to bubble, scoop about ¼ cup of the batter and drop onto the surface. Repeat for as many pancakes as will fit comfortably. Cook until bubbles form on the surface, then flip with a spatula and cook until golden brown on both sides. Transfer to a baking sheet or platter and cover to keep warm. Repeat with the remaining batter, adding more butter as needed.

To serve, stack the pancakes on individual serving plates. Top with the warm berries and whipped mascarpone.

Banana Bread

MAKES TWO 9 BY 5-INCH LOAVES

2½ sticks (20 tablespoons) unsalted butter at room temperature, plus more for pans

4 cups plus 2 tablespoons (1 pound, 2 ounces) all-purpose flour, plus more for pans

2 teaspoons kosher salt

2 teaspoons baking soda

1¾ cups granulated sugar

8 to 9 ripe bananas, pureed

3 large eggs

1 teaspoon vanilla extract

1 heaping cup chopped, toasted walnuts or pecans (optional)

Chef's Tip: Instead of tossing spotty or browning bananas, freeze them to use later. The skin will blacken but the fruit will be good for purees, smoothies, or this banana bread.

I STARTED MAKING this quick bread when our first son, Hudson, was quite young. After his brother, Ethan, came along, we discovered he had a nut allergy, so I often omit the nuts and the recipe doesn't suffer. It's a good use for overripe bananas, which I throw in the freezer. When I've accumulated eight or nine, I defrost them and make these loaves. –*Lisa Sewall*

Preheat the oven to 350°F.

Butter and flour two 9 by 5–inch loaf pans.

In a medium bowl, mix together the 4 cups plus 2 tablespoons flour, salt, and baking soda and set aside.

In the bowl of a stand mixer fitted with the paddle attachment, cream the 2½ sticks butter and sugar on medium speed until light and fluffy, about 5 minutes. Scrape down the sides of the bowl and add the banana puree, eggs, and vanilla and mix to combine on medium speed. (The batter may look broken at this point.) Add the dry ingredients and mix on low speed until just combined. Fold in the nuts by hand with a rubber spatula, if using.

Divide the batter evenly between the 2 loaf pans and use a rubber spatula to smooth the tops. Bake until golden brown and a cake tester inserted in the middle of the loaves comes out clean, about 1 hour.

Let the breads cool in their pans on racks for 15 minutes, then turn the breads out of the pans and set on a rack until completely cool. Wrap the loaves and refrigerate for up to 1 week or freeze.

Berry and Banana Smoothies SERVES 4 TO 6

I LIKE A GOOD SMOOTHIE and it's a great thing to feed kids in the morning. You don't need to overthink it: Just blend a few fresh ingredients for a great start to the day. I prefer to keep it simple with berries and a banana, but you can use ripe peaches, mango, or any other favorite. I use fresh fruit but frozen works just as well.

Place the ingredients in a blender and puree until smooth.

1 ripe banana, peeled

1 cup sliced strawberries

½ cup blueberries

Juice of 2 oranges (about ¼ cup)

¼ cup Greek yogurt

1 cup ice cubes

Chef's Tip: To turn this into a milkshake, substitute 1 cup vanilla ice cream for the ice cubes and yogurt—I won't judge you if you make that your breakfast.

Chapter 2
Lunch

I recently read that "lunch is the most important meal—between breakfast and dinner." I couldn't agree more with this sentiment. We pack it for our kids to take to school. We use it as a chance to take a work break in the middle of the day. By its nature, lunch is social. During our school years, we eat lunch in a cafeteria with our friends, and at work many adults do the same. I highly recommend taking the time to make a great lunch at home occasionally and inviting friends to share it with you. Just like when we were kids, it's better when shared.

I will give the same advice for lunch as I would for breakfast or dinner: Do some prep ahead of time so that it's easy to pull together. You should spend more time enjoying lunch than making it.

I like to keep it simple with dishes like Chilled Soba Noodles with Shrimp and Peanut Sauce (page 54) or Roasted Vegetable Pita Sandwiches with Carrot Hummus and Dill Crema (page 37), but there's always room in my week for a great sandwich—the Roast Beef and Caramelized Onion Sandwiches (page 51) and the Fried Chicken Sandwiches with Pickles, Quick Slaw, and Hot Sauce Aïoli (page 48) are two of my favorites. And for a solid make-ahead option, you can't go wrong with an Egg Salad on Toasted Baguette (page 46). Whatever you make, take the time to enjoy it.

Sweet Potato, Broccoli, and Cheddar Quiche

MAKES ONE 10-INCH QUICHE, ABOUT 4 SERVINGS

ONCE YOU LEARN TO MAKE a basic tart shell crust you can fill it with all sorts of ingredients. Quiche is a good catchall for using what you have on hand, since you can fill a quiche with almost anything. The trick is making sure everything is cooked well in advance so that when you combine it with the eggs, there isn't any excess moisture, which would prevent the eggs from setting. After it's baked, make sure to give it time to cool down to room temperature, which makes it easier to slice. And be sure to use a quiche pan with a removable bottom. I like serving this with the Simple Greens and Herb Salad from page 75 to make it a complete meal.

For the crust, place the flours, butter, and salt in the bowl of a food processor fitted with the metal blade and pulse until the mixture looks like sand. Add the water, a little at a time, pulsing until the dough forms a rough ball. Scrape the dough onto a work surface and knead by hand until it comes together. You may need a little extra flour if it's sticky. Wrap the dough in plastic and refrigerate for at least 2 hours.

For the filling, peel the sweet potato and dice into ½-inch pieces. Rinse under cold water, then set on a paper towel–lined plate and pat dry. In a large sauté pan, heat the olive oil over medium heat and add the sweet potato. Cook until it just begins to soften, 7 to 8 minutes. Add the broccoli florets and continue to cook, stirring occasionally, until the broccoli begins to soften, 3 to 4 additional minutes. Add the shallot and garlic. Continue cooking until the shallots are softened and starting to color lightly, about 2 additional minutes. Remove from the heat and set aside to cool.

Meanwhile, remove the dough from the refrigerator and let it sit at room temperature for about 5 minutes. Lightly flour the work surface and use a rolling pin to roll the dough into a ¼-inch-thick round. Carefully transfer the dough to a 10-inch quiche pan with a removable bottom. Press the dough evenly into the base and inside edges of the pan. Press any excess dough off around the top edges and use it to patch any holes or tears. Make sure the dough is firmly pressed into the edge where the base meets the shell. Loosely cover the dough with plastic wrap and refrigerate for 1 hour.

Preheat the oven to 350°F.

Line the dough with parchment paper and fill with dried beans or pie weights (this keeps the dough from puffing up). Place the quiche pan

CRUST

1 cup all-purpose flour, plus more for dusting

¼ cup whole wheat flour

1 stick (8 tablespoons) cold unsalted butter, cut into cubes

1 teaspoon kosher salt

¼ cup ice water

FILLING

1 medium sweet potato

2 tablespoons extra-virgin olive oil

1 cup broccoli florets

1 small shallot, minced

1 tablespoon minced garlic

½ cup shredded cheddar cheese

3 large eggs

1½ cups half-and-half

2 teaspoons kosher salt

1 teaspoon freshly ground black pepper

on a baking sheet and bake for 20 minutes. Remove from the oven and carefully remove the parchment with the beans. Place the shell back in the oven for 7 additional minutes. Remove and let cool.

Once the shell has cooled, transfer the sautéed sweet potato and broccoli mixture to the shell, spreading the vegetables evenly over the bottom. Sprinkle half of the cheese on top.

In a medium bowl, whisk together the eggs, half-and-half, salt, and pepper. Carefully pour the egg mixture over the vegetables, leaving about 1 inch free at the top of the shell. Sprinkle the remaining cheese on top and bake for 20 minutes. Rotate the pan and bake for an additional 20 minutes. Raise the oven temperature to 450°F and continue baking until the top is lightly browned, about 7 minutes. The filling should feel firm to the touch but still have a little wiggle to it. Remove the quiche from the oven and let cool to room temperature before removing the bottom and sides of the pan.

Roasted Vegetable Pita Sandwiches with Carrot Hummus and Dill Crema

MAKES 12 SMALL SANDWICHES

CONSIDER THIS A SANDWICH for every cooking level. You can make all of the elements yourself, including the pita breads (I include a recipe for them on page 39), or you can sub in a few high-quality store-bought ingredients, like pita bread and hummus. I personally love to have this carrot hummus on hand since it's a great snack any time of day.

For the hummus, preheat the oven to 350°F.

On a baking sheet lined with parchment paper, toss the carrots with the olive oil, turmeric, cumin, and coriander. Season with salt and pepper. Roast until the carrots are soft, about 15 minutes. Remove from the oven but leave the oven on for roasting the other vegetables. Let the carrots cool for about 10 minutes. Transfer the carrots to a blender, scraping the paper with a flexible rubber spatula to get all the spices and olive oil.

To the blender, add the chickpeas, garlic confit, lemon juice, and tahini, and season with salt and pepper. Pulse a few times. Add 1 to 2 tablespoons of cold water and continue to puree, adding more water as needed to create a smooth texture, though the finished hummus should be fairly thick. Transfer to a bowl and refrigerate until ready to use.

For the crema, in a medium bowl, fold together the crème fraîche, dill, and lemon zest and juice. Season with salt and pepper and set aside.

For the roasted vegetables, on a baking sheet toss the zucchini and red pepper with the olive oil and season with salt and pepper. Roast for 15 minutes. Remove and let cool completely. Add the roasted vegetables to the bowl of crema, season with salt and pepper, and stir to combine.

To assemble, cut each pita in half and open each piece to form a pocket. Spread about 1 tablespoon of the carrot hummus on the inside of a pita half and then place a few leaves of arugula in the bottom. Layer the roasted vegetables inside the pita half and top with a few tomatoes. Repeat with remaining bread, hummus, and vegetables.

HUMMUS

1 cup sliced carrots

½ cup extra-virgin olive oil

¼ teaspoon ground turmeric

¼ teaspoon ground cumin

¼ teaspoon ground coriander

Kosher salt and freshly ground black pepper

1 cup Cooked Chickpeas (page 230)

1 tablespoon plus 1 teaspoon Garlic Confit (page 224)

3 tablespoons freshly squeezed lemon juice

2 tablespoons tahini

CREMA

½ cup crème fraîche

1 tablespoon chopped fresh dill

Finely grated zest of ½ lemon

1 tablespoon freshly squeezed lemon juice

Kosher salt and freshly ground black pepper

VEGETABLES

1 small zucchini, sliced ¼ inch thick

1 red bell pepper, seeded and cut into ¼-inch strips

3 tablespoons extra-virgin olive oil

Kosher salt and freshly ground black pepper

½ cup arugula

1 cup halved medley cherry tomatoes

6 Pita Breads (page 39)

Pita Breads MAKES 6 BREADS

PITA IS NOT HARD TO MAKE *and gives a great sense of accomplishment. I prefer using a cast-iron skillet to cook these because it retains heat so well, but any type of skillet (except for nonstick) will work. I make the dough by hand, because I enjoy the act of kneading—and this is a soft dough— but a stand mixer works just as well.*

In a mixing bowl, whisk together the water, yeast, and sugar. Let sit for 20 minutes; it should start to froth as the yeast activates. Add the 2 tablespoons olive oil and salt and stir with a wooden spoon. Add 2 cups of the all-purpose flour and the wheat flour and stir until the dough forms a ball. Use some of the remaining flour to dust the work surface. Turn the dough onto the surface and knead until it comes together into a tender dough, about 5 minutes. The dough should be moist, but if it is so sticky that it continues to stick to the surface, add a little flour at a time.

Return the dough to the mixing bowl and cover tightly with plastic wrap. Proof in a warm spot until it doubles in size, about 1 hour. Turn the dough back onto the floured work surface and divide into 6 equal pieces. Shape each piece into a ball. Set aside and cover loosely. Allow the balls to proof until they are slightly risen, 30 to 45 minutes; when pressed with a finger, the dough should spring back. (The dough balls don't need to double in size.)

Preheat the oven to 350°F.

Roll each piece of dough into a circle ¼ to ½ inch thick. Set aside—do not stack—and cover loosely, and allow to rest for 20 to 30 minutes. Place a cast-iron skillet over medium-high heat and brush the pan with a little olive oil. Once the pan is hot, add one dough circle to the pan. The edges should start to bubble as the dough firms up. Cook until the bottom is light brown and the pita feels light but still flexible, 3 to 4 minutes. Flip the pita and cook until there's a little color on the other side. Transfer the pita to a rack set on a baking sheet. Repeat with the remaining dough.

Transfer the baking sheet to the oven and bake the pitas for 6 minutes to cook through. Let the pitas cool on the rack for a few minutes before using.

1 cup warm water

2¼ teaspoons (1 packet) active dry yeast

¾ teaspoon granulated sugar

2 tablespoons extra-virgin olive oil, plus more for pan

2 tablespoons kosher salt

2½ cups all-purpose flour

1 cup whole wheat flour

Egg Sandwiches with Prosciutto, Arugula, and Tomato MAKES 4 SANDWICHES

4 sesame seed slider rolls

¼ cup extra-virgin olive oil

¼ cup finely grated Parmesan cheese

¼ cup Basil Pesto (page 167)

1 cup arugula leaves

8 slices prosciutto

1 beefsteak tomato, sliced

4 Sunny-Side Up Eggs (page 228)

Kosher salt and freshly ground black pepper

1 teaspoon chili flakes (optional)

WHEN I WAS A KID, one of my favorite breakfasts to eat either at home or from the local deli was a fried egg, ham, and cheese sandwich on a roll. It became a staple during my teen years. Consider this the cheffed-up version, with the salty kick of prosciutto and sharp tang of arugula. If you prefer a ham-and-cheddar version, feel free to swap those out for the prosciutto and Parmesan. You could also make these with the Seeded Sandwich Rolls (page 52), which will be a bit larger than the slider rolls. It's the perfect lunch or brunch item to make on the go.

Slice the rolls in half. Set a sauté pan or a griddle over medium heat. Add the olive oil and place two of the rolls cut-sides down in the pan. Toast until just browned, 2 to 3 minutes. Set aside and repeat with the remaining rolls.

Place the rolls on a cutting board toasted sides up. Evenly divide the Parmesan among the warm rolls. On the bottom halves of the rolls, build sandwiches: spread pesto on the bottoms, followed by handfuls of arugula, the prosciutto, the tomato slices, and the sunny-side up eggs on top. (Try to keep the yolks at the center of the sandwiches.) Season the eggs with salt, pepper, and chili flakes, if using. Cover the sandwiches with the tops of the rolls and slice each in half before serving.

Pesto-Marinated Tomatoes on Toasted Baguette SERVES 4

THIS IS A GREAT SNACK or light entrée. Serve it with the Simple Green and Herb Salad (page 75) for the perfect lunch. I call for small cherry tomatoes here (use a sharp knife to cut them), but larger tomatoes will also work, as long as you core and dice them. If you like heat, swap jalapeño peppers for the Fresnos, which are red and more sweet than spicy. Prepare the cream cheese mixture and pickle the Fresno peppers a day or two in advance and this becomes an easy dish to pull together quickly.

In a bowl, combine the tomatoes with the pesto and season with salt and pepper. Refrigerate until about 15 minutes before you're ready to serve.

In a small saucepan, combine the vinegar and sugar, bring to a boil, and simmer until the sugar is dissolved. Place the pepper slices in a heatproof bowl and pour the vinegar mixture over them. Allow to cool to room temperature, then drain off the liquid and discard.

Place the cream cheese in a mixing bowl and add the scallions. Season with salt and pepper. Fold the mixture together until completely combined.

Preheat the oven to 350°F.

Brush one side of the baguette slices with the olive oil and place in a single layer on a baking sheet. Toast in the oven until lightly browned, about 7 minutes. Remove and let cool slightly; rub a garlic half over the tops of the toasted bread.

To serve, spread some of the cream cheese mixture on one side of each baguette slice and arrange on a platter. Spoon the tomatoes over the cream cheese, and top with the pickled peppers.

1 pint medley cherry tomatoes, halved

¼ cup Basil Pesto (page 167)

Kosher salt and freshly ground black pepper

¼ cup rice wine vinegar

¼ cup granulated sugar

3 Fresno peppers, seeded and sliced into thin rounds

½ cup cream cheese, room temperature

6 scallions, green parts only, thinly sliced

1 baguette, sliced on an angle about ½ inch thick (about 8 slices)

¼ cup extra-virgin olive oil

1 clove garlic, halved

Lettuce Cups with Pickled Beets and Apples

MAKES 16 CUPS

2 tablespoons white wine

1 tablespoon honey

¼ cup raisins

2 heads romaine lettuce

1 cup Basic Pickled Beets
(page 225), cut into
small dice

1 honeycrisp apple, cored,
peeled, and cut into small
dice

1 tablespoon extra-virgin
olive oil

Kosher salt and freshly ground
black pepper

½ cup plain Greek yogurt

¼ cup pine nuts, toasted

THIS IS A GOOD RECIPE to prep in advance and assemble once you're ready to eat. And it's versatile, too—you can either layer the yogurt into the lettuce cup before putting everything else in or mix the ingredients right into the yogurt before spooning it on (this makes it easier if you want everyone to serve themselves). Be sure to dice the beets small for this recipe—and feel free to use a mix of red and yellow. I like the pop of color that yellow beets offer.

In a small saucepan, combine the wine, 3 tablespoons water, and honey and bring to a boil. Add the raisins, cover, and remove from the heat. Let sit until the liquid is cool. Drain well.

Cut off the roots of the heads of lettuce and separate the leaves—you should have about 16 sturdy leaves. Rinse the leaves under cold water to remove any dirt and spread on kitchen towels in a single layer. Pat dry.

In a bowl, combine the beets, plumped raisins, apple, and olive oil. Season lightly with salt and pepper. To serve, place 1 heaping teaspoon of yogurt in the center of each lettuce leaf and spoon a little of the beet mixture on top using the yogurt as glue to help hold everything in place. Sprinkle pine nuts on top and serve.

Egg Salad on Toasted Baguette SERVES 4

DON'T SLEEP ON EGG SALAD just because it's familiar—it can be delicious, especially if you've been to a nearby farmer's market for fresh eggs and a local bakery for a fresh baguette. If you don't have fresh dill, tarragon makes a great substitute, but don't skip the fresh herbs, as they make this shine.

Place the eggs in a medium saucepan with cold water to cover and the 2 tablespoons salt. Bring to a boil, then reduce to a gentle simmer for 1 minute. Remove the pan from the heat and cover with a tight-fitting lid. Let sit for 12 minutes. Drain the water and run the eggs under cold water until the shells are cool enough to handle. Peel the eggs and refrigerate until fully chilled.

Once chilled, cut the eggs in half and place in a mixing bowl. Add the mayonnaise and mash the eggs with a fork. (I like to leave a few larger pieces of egg in the mix.) Gently fold in the pickle, mustard, celery, 1 teaspoon chopped dill, lemon juice, and Tabasco, and season with salt and pepper. Refrigerate until ready to serve.

Preheat the oven to 350°F (or use a toaster oven).

Spread the garlic confit on one side of each baguette slice. Place the slices on a baking sheet and toast in the oven for 8 minutes. Allow to cool slightly, then spread egg salad on top of each slice. Garnish with the paprika and dill leaves, and season with additional black pepper.

6 large eggs

2 tablespoons kosher salt, plus more to taste

¾ cup mayonnaise

1 tablespoon minced dill pickle

1 tablespoon Dijon mustard

1 rib celery, minced

1 teaspoon chopped fresh dill, plus a few whole leaves for garnish

1 tablespoon freshly squeezed lemon juice

½ teaspoon Tabasco sauce

Freshly ground black pepper

¼ cup Garlic Confit (page 224)

1 baguette, sliced on an angle about ½ inch thick (about 8 slices)

½ teaspoon smoked paprika

Chef's Tip: For easy-to-assemble garlic bread, spread Garlic Confit (page 224) on slices of baguette, then toast in a 350°F oven for 8 minutes.

Fried Chicken Sandwiches with Pickles, Quick Slaw, and Hot Sauce Aïoli MAKES 4 SANDWICHES

4 boneless, skinless chicken thighs

½ cup buttermilk

½ cup sliced dill pickles, plus 2 tablespoons reserved pickle juice

¼ cup Tabasco sauce

1½ cups all-purpose flour

1 teaspoon paprika

1 teaspoon mustard powder

½ teaspoon garlic powder

½ teaspoon onion powder

Kosher salt and freshly ground black pepper

Canola oil for frying

1 tablespoon Garlic Confit (page 224)

½ cup mayonnaise

1¼ cups Quick Slaw (recipe follows)

4 brioche buns, halved and lightly toasted

FOR THE QUICK SLAW

1 cup thinly sliced Napa cabbage

1 medium carrot, grated on the large holes of a box grater

¼ cup thinly sliced red onion

2 tablespoons apple cider vinegar

1 teaspoon granulated sugar

1 teaspoon kosher salt

¼ teaspoon celery salt

Chef's Tip: Aïoli is garlic mayonnaise. Use your favorite mayo as the base, combine it with Garlic Confit (page 224), and fold in whatever other ingredients you care to add, like herbs, spices, or hot sauce.

MAKING FRIED CHICKEN at home is easy with a small counter-top fryer. A cast-iron skillet or other heavy-bottomed pan will work, too—just be careful when moving the pan around after you're done cooking. (I move mine to a back burner until the oil is fully cooled.) Use chicken thighs when making sandwiches, since they have more flavor than breasts.

Trim any large pieces of fat from the thighs. Place the thighs between two pieces of plastic wrap and use a mallet to pound lightly so the meat is an even thickness. Place in a bowl and add the buttermilk, pickle juice, and 2 tablespoons Tabasco; toss to coat. Refrigerate, covered, for 1 hour.

In a shallow bowl, whisk together the flour, paprika, mustard powder, garlic powder, and onion powder, and season with salt and pepper.

To a countertop deep fryer or a heavy-bottomed pot or Dutch oven, add several inches of canola oil—enough to cover the chicken pieces. Heat the oil to 350°F. Working quickly, remove one chicken thigh from the buttermilk and dredge in the flour mixture to coat. Repeat the process, dipping the chicken into the buttermilk again and then back into the flour. Gently shake off any excess flour and carefully place into the oil. Repeat with the remaining thighs. Fry until golden brown and crisp, 5 to 7 minutes, turning them halfway through cooking. Once the pieces are golden brown and crispy, use a skimmer to transfer them to a paper towel–lined platter to drain. Season immediately with salt and pepper.

Place the garlic confit in a medium bowl along with the remaining 2 tablespoons Tabasco and mash with a fork to form a paste. Whisk in the mayonnaise. Add the slaw to the bowl and stir to combine.

To assemble the sandwiches, start with the dressed slaw on a bottom bun, then place a piece of fried chicken on top, followed by the pickles. Cover with the top bun. Repeat with the remaining buns, slaw, chicken, and pickles and serve immediately.

Quick Slaw MAKES 1¼ CUPS

In a large bowl, combine all ingredients and stir well. Let sit for 1 hour. Drain off any excess liquid before using in the recipe.

Roast Beef and Caramelized Onion Sandwiches

MAKES 6 SANDWICHES

I GREW UP EATING roast beef sandwiches from the local deli. Thinly sliced, rare roast beef on a deli roll with lots of mayo is still one of my favorite lunches. I cheffed up this recipe a little bit, and even if you love a deli sandwich as much as I do, it's super satisfying to craft these from scratch. For the beef, I like to use a cut called the teres major (it also goes by petite tender). It's flavorful and just the right size for sandwich slices. If you can't find that cut, feel free to use an eye round or bottom round roast.

For the roast beef, preheat the oven to 450°F. In a large bowl, whisk together the paprika, salt, pepper, and oil. Place the steak in the bowl and roll it around in the oil mixture. Transfer the meat to a wire rack set on top of a baking sheet and pour any seasoned oil that remains in the bowl over the top, gently rubbing it into the steak. Roast for 10 minutes, then reduce the temperature to 275°F and roast until an instant-read thermometer reads 125°F, about 15 additional minutes. Remove from the oven and allow to rest for 30 minutes. With a sharp knife, shave the meat into very thin slices. (The slices don't need to be perfect or even.) Raise the oven temperature to 350°F (or plan to use a toaster oven to warm up the rolls).

Meanwhile, for the onions, in a large sauté pan, heat the canola oil over medium heat. Add the onions. Use a wooden spoon or spatula to cook, stirring frequently, for 3 to 4 minutes. Reduce the heat to low and continue cooking, stirring occasionally and scraping the bottom of the pan to keep the onions from sticking or burning. Cook until the onions take on a caramel color and smell sweet, about 20 minutes. Remove the pan from the heat and allow to cool to room temperature.

To assemble the sandwiches, warm the rolls in the 350°F oven for 3 minutes. Remove and slice each roll in half. Spread about 1 tablespoon of the aïoli on the top and bottom of each roll. On the bottom half, spread a layer of caramelized onion. Top with a layer of sliced beef and season with a little salt and pepper. Add 1 slice of tomato and a few romaine leaves to each sandwich and cover with the top of the roll. Serve immediately.

ROAST BEEF

1 teaspoon paprika

1 tablespoon kosher salt

1 teaspoon freshly ground black pepper

¼ cup extra-virgin olive oil

2 pounds teres major steak (or eye round or bottom round roast)

ONIONS

3 tablespoons canola oil

2 large Spanish onions, thinly sliced

Kosher salt and freshly ground black pepper

ASSEMBLY

6 Seeded Sandwich Rolls (recipe follows)

¾ cup Black Pepper Aïoli (recipe follows)

Kosher salt and freshly ground black pepper

1 beefsteak tomato, sliced

1 small head romaine lettuce, divided into leaves

Seeded Sandwich Rolls   MAKES 6 ROLLS

¾ cup warm water

2 teaspoons dry yeast

1 tablespoon honey

2 large eggs

2 tablespoons extra-virgin olive oil

1½ teaspoons kosher salt

3 cups all-purpose flour

1 teaspoon poppy seeds

1 teaspoon sesame seeds

1 teaspoon sea salt

In the bowl of a stand mixer fitted with a dough hook, add the warm water and, by hand, whisk in the yeast and honey. Let sit for 15 minutes, until the mixture becomes frothy. In order, add 1 egg, the olive oil, salt, and flour. Mix on medium speed until the dough comes together into a firm ball, about 8 minutes. Cover the bowl and let sit in a warm place until the dough doubles in size, about 1 hour.

Divide the dough into 6 equal pieces (about 4 ounces each) and roll into balls. Roll the balls flat with a rolling pin so they are about ½ inch thick and circular. Place the rolls on a baking sheet and cover with plastic wrap. Allow the rolls to proof until they've more than doubled in size, 35 to 45 minutes.

Preheat a convection oven to 375°F. (If using a standard oven, set it to the same temperature; the cooking time will be longer.)

In a small bowl, whisk the remaining egg and use a pastry brush to brush the top of each roll with egg. Combine the seeds and sea salt in a small bowl and evenly sprinkle the mixture on top of the rolls.

Bake in the convection oven for 8 minutes (10 minutes in a standard oven). Rotate the baking sheet and reduce the temperature to 350°F. Bake for an additional 6 minutes (7 to 10 minutes in a standard oven). Remove the rolls from the oven and allow to cool. The rolls may be stored in a sealed container at room temperature for up to 3 days.

Black Pepper Aïoli   MAKES 1¼ CUPS

2 teaspoons Garlic Confit (page 224)

1 cup mayonnaise

1 tablespoon freshly squeezed lemon juice

1 teaspoon freshly ground black pepper

Kosher salt

Place the garlic confit in a medium bowl and whisk in the mayonnaise, lemon juice, 3 tablespoons room-temperature water, and the black pepper. Season with salt to taste. Refrigerate until ready to use.

Rice and Quinoa Bowl with Roasted Kale and Marinated Cucumber SERVES 4

MY WIFE LISA INTRODUCED ME to quinoa about thirty years ago, but I didn't think about it much until I saw it again in a Charlie Trotter cookbook. Quinoa is a healthy, ancient seed that eats like a grain and is a great source of protein and flavor. Sitting down to a plain bowl of quinoa doesn't do it for me—quinoa needs to be paired with other ingredients. This dish can be eaten either warm or cold. Make it in advance for an easy weekday lunch. Pro tip: Spend a little extra on good balsamic vinegar. It makes a difference.

Rinse the quinoa under cold water, then transfer to a medium saucepan. Add cold water to cover by 1 inch and some salt, and place over medium heat. Simmer until tender, about 15 minutes. Drain the quinoa and spread it on a baking sheet to cool.

Rinse the saucepan and add the brown rice. Add cold water to cover by 1 inch and some salt, and place over medium heat. Simmer until tender, about 30 minutes. Drain the rice and spread it on a baking sheet to cool.

Preheat the oven to 350°F.

On a baking sheet, toss the kale with a few drops of the olive oil and season with salt and pepper. Roast until the kale is wilted and the edges begin to get a little crispy, about 10 minutes. Remove and let cool.

Meanwhile, peel, seed, and thinly slice the cucumber and place in a medium bowl with the tomatoes and red onion. Toss with the remaining olive oil and balsamic vinegar and season with salt. Refrigerate for about 30 minutes.

When ready to serve, transfer the cooked quinoa and rice to a large nonstick sauté pan and place over medium-low heat. Stir in the roasted kale, lemon zest, and lemon juice and cook, stirring occasionally, until heated through. Taste and adjust seasoning, then transfer to a serving dish. Stir the parsley into the cucumbers and spoon the mixture and all of its liquid over the rice and quinoa. Cut the avocado in half, remove the pit, and slice the flesh. Layer the slices over the quinoa salad and season the avocado with a little salt.

1 cup red quinoa

Kosher salt

½ cup brown rice

2 cups torn, stemmed curly kale

¼ cup extra-virgin olive oil

Freshly ground black pepper

1 English cucumber

1 cup halved medley cherry tomatoes

¼ cup thinly sliced red onion

2 tablespoons balsamic vinegar

Finely grated zest and juice of 1 lemon

2 tablespoons chopped flat-leaf parsley leaves

1 ripe avocado

Chef's Tip: After cooking grains, I prefer to spread the drained grains on a baking sheet to cool. This keeps the grains from clumping and allows them to dry evenly and completely.

Chilled Soba Noodles with Shrimp and Peanut Sauce **SERVES 4**

SOBA NOODLES ARE MADE from buckwheat, and their hearty flavor shines whether they're served hot or cold. This cold dish travels well, so consider it for your next picnic. The peanut sauce shouldn't be too thick—just enough to coat the noodles. And be sure to reserve some of the sauce to serve on the side.

For the peanut sauce, in a mixing bowl whisk together the peanut butter and water until combined. Whisk in the remaining ingredients. Set aside or refrigerate until ready to use.

For the noodles, bring a large pot of salted water to a boil and add the noodles. Cook until tender, 4 to 7 minutes. (Check the packaging, as cooking times vary.) Drain and transfer to a large mixing bowl. Add the olive oil and toss to combine. Refrigerate until chilled.

In a sauté pan over medium-high heat, add the canola oil. Season the shrimp with salt and pepper and place in the pan. Sear the shrimp on both sides until they are cooked through, 1 to 2 minutes per side. Remove the shrimp from the pan and squeeze half of the lime over them. Set aside.

To the bowl of noodles, add three-quarters of the peanut sauce and toss to combine, making sure the noodles are coated. Transfer the noodles to a serving dish and top with the carrot, cucumber, radishes, peppers, if using, and peanuts. Arrange the shrimp on top and squeeze the other half of the lime over the dish. Garnish with the Thai basil leaves and togarashi. Serve the remaining peanut sauce on the side.

PEANUT SAUCE

½ cup smooth natural peanut butter

½ cup hot water

2 tablespoons rice wine vinegar

2 tablespoons soy sauce

2 tablespoons lime juice

1 tablespoon grated ginger

1 tablespoon toasted sesame oil

1 tablespoon sriracha

NOODLES AND ASSEMBLY

Kosher salt

8 ounces soba noodles

2 tablespoons extra-virgin olive oil

2 tablespoons canola oil

1 pound (size U25/30) shrimp, peeled and deveined

Freshly ground black pepper

1 lime, halved

1 small carrot, shredded

1 small English cucumber, peeled, seeded, and sliced

2 breakfast radishes, thinly sliced

¼ cup Pickled Jalapeño Peppers, optional (page 99)

½ cup salted roasted peanuts, crushed

12 Thai basil leaves

½ teaspoon togarashi

Chapter 3
Soups and Salads

The sensation of sitting before a warm bowl of soup on a cold day. The elegance of sipping broth from a spoon at a fancy restaurant. Soup might seem simple, but it has its place in both the finest and the most rustic of dining rooms. Being able to make a good bowl of soup is a superpower—once you master a recipe, you can take someone's day from basic to unforgettable. It's all about seasoning as you go and learning when to make something in advance to let the flavors develop. Plus, soup-making is a great space for celebrating humble ingredients and using up what you have. The White Bean and Ham Hock Stew on page 68 needs nothing more than crusty bread, while the Summer Gazpacho with Grilled Shrimp and Avocado on page 60 should be part of a colorful summer spread.

I combined soups and salads in this chapter because many of them can go together to make a full meal—consider serving the Asparagus Soup with Poached Eggs from page 58 and the Pickled Beets with Creamy Goat Cheese and Toasted Almonds from page 80. Salads are all about the freshness of the ingredients, so make sure you're finding the best—this is the time to be picky.

Asparagus Soup with Poached Eggs SERVES 4

THIS IS A LOVELY SOUP, both for its bright color and for the way it shows off the flavor of asparagus. It requires an extra step or two, but the result is worth it. Don't skip the eggs, which add richness and balance out the garlicky bread. Or omit the eggs and the bread and serve this chilled with a dollop of crème fraîche.

Prepare an ice bath as on page 225.

Cut off the bottom few inches of the asparagus spears and reserve. In a pot of boiling water, blanch the asparagus tops for 3 to 4 minutes. Transfer to the ice bath to cool. Remove the asparagus from the ice bath and refrigerate.

In a medium saucepan, heat the canola oil over medium heat and add the shallot and garlic. Sauté until they begin to color lightly. Add the reserved asparagus stems, vegetable stock, and heavy cream. Bring to a boil, then reduce heat to medium-low. Add the thyme and simmer for 30 minutes. Remove from the heat and allow to cool to room temperature.

Strain the soup through a fine-mesh strainer into a medium bowl. (Discard solids.) Stir in the lemon juice, then refrigerate until cool, about 45 minutes. Transfer the cooled soup to a blender along with the blanched asparagus tops. Blend until smooth. Pour the soup into a clean saucepan and season with salt and pepper. Warm over medium heat, stirring frequently.

Meanwhile, preheat the oven to 350°F.

Spread the garlic confit on top of the baguette slices. Place on a baking sheet and bake for 12 minutes. When ready to serve, place a slice of baguette in the bottom of each serving bowl and carefully place a poached egg on top. Pour the soup around the egg and garnish with the Aleppo pepper. Serve hot.

1 bunch asparagus

1 tablespoon canola oil

1 shallot, sliced

1 clove garlic, chopped

1½ cups vegetable stock

1 cup heavy cream

3 sprigs thyme

1 teaspoon freshly squeezed lemon juice

Kosher salt and freshly ground black pepper

1 tablespoon Garlic Confit (page 224)

4 slices baguette

4 Poached Eggs (page 228)

½ teaspoon Aleppo pepper

Summer Gazpacho with Grilled Shrimp and Avocado

SERVES 4

SOUP

4 beefsteak tomatoes, cored and chopped, juices reserved

1 small cucumber, sliced

1 small red bell pepper, stemmed, seeded, and chopped

1 jalapeño or Fresno pepper, stemmed, seeded, and chopped

1 small red onion, chopped

1 clove garlic, crushed

½ cup freshly squeezed lime juice

2 tablespoons roughly chopped cilantro leaves

Kosher salt and freshly ground black pepper

GARNISH

16 shrimp (size U21/25), peeled and deveined

Extra-virgin olive oil for brushing and drizzling

Kosher salt and freshly ground black pepper

1 tablespoon chopped cilantro leaves

1 cup yellow cherry tomatoes, halved

2 ripe avocados

2 tablespoons freshly squeezed lime juice

GAZPACHO SHOULD BE MADE at the peak of tomato season. The base of this soup can be readied a day ahead—let it marinate overnight for best results. And make sure you use all the juice from the chopped tomatoes. I like to use U21/25 shrimp—the code indicates the size of the shrimp (in this case, it's 21 to 25 shrimp per pound).

For the soup, in a bowl, combine all the ingredients, including the tomato juices, and season with salt and pepper. Refrigerate, covered, for at least 3 hours and up to 12 hours. Transfer to a blender and puree until smooth. Refrigerate until ready to serve.

For the garnish, preheat a grill to medium-high heat.

Brush the shrimp with a little olive oil and season with salt and pepper. Place on the hot grill and char until just cooked through, about 3 minutes per side. Remove and allow to cool. Once cool, slice the shrimp into bite-size pieces and place in a bowl with the cilantro and cherry tomatoes. Season with salt and pepper and stir to combine.

Split the avocados and remove the pits. Scoop the flesh from the peels and place in a bowl with the lime juice. Season with salt and pepper and mash with a fork until the lime juice is mixed in and the avocado is in small pieces.

To serve, divide the gazpacho among individual serving bowls. Place a scoop of the avocado mixture in the center of each bowl and spoon the shrimp mixture on top of the avocado. Drizzle with olive oil and serve.

Roasted Parsnip Soup with Brown Butter

SERVES 4

I LOVE PARSNIPS because they're so versatile. I especially enjoy them roasted, which gives them a rich, warming flavor. Be sure to cut the parsnips into similarly sized pieces so that they cook evenly. If you have a very powerful blender, you can skip the straining, but better safe than sorry. Like many soups, this one tastes better if you make it a day in advance and allow the flavors to combine and develop.

Preheat the oven to 425°F.

On a baking sheet, toss the parsnips with 2 tablespoons of the canola oil. Roast until they're colored slightly but not fully cooked, about 10 minutes. Remove from the oven and reduce the oven temperature to 350°F.

Meanwhile, in a large saucepan or stockpot, heat the remaining 2 tablespoons canola oil over medium heat. Add the onion and celery and cook until they begin to soften and color lightly. Add the garlic confit, rosemary, and roasted parsnips and stir to combine. Add the stock and bring to a boil. Reduce the heat and simmer for 25 minutes. Stir in the cream and simmer for 15 additional minutes. Stir in the vinegar and season with salt and pepper to taste. Remove from the heat and allow to cool for 15 minutes. Use an immersion blender to puree the soup (or carefully transfer to a blender and puree in batches). Strain the soup, then taste and adjust seasoning. Return the soup to the pot and warm over medium-low heat, stirring frequently.

Place the bread on a baking sheet and toss with the olive oil. Season with salt and pepper. Toast in the oven for 8 minutes. While the bread is toasting, place the butter in a small sauté pan over medium heat. As the butter melts it will start to separate and bubble; stir while it melts. Once it is lightly browned, remove the pan from the heat and let it sit for 5 minutes. (It will continue to brown as it sits.)

To serve, ladle the soup into serving bowls. Drizzle a little of the brown butter over the top and scatter on the toasted sourdough.

5 medium parsnips, peeled and chopped into 2-inch pieces

¼ cup canola oil

1 small Spanish onion, thinly sliced

1 rib celery, sliced

2 tablespoons Garlic Confit (page 224)

1 teaspoon chopped rosemary

3 cups vegetable stock

1 cup heavy cream

1 tablespoon sherry vinegar

Kosher salt and freshly ground black pepper

1 small loaf sourdough bread, crusts removed and torn into chunks (about 2 cups)

¼ cup extra-virgin olive oil

4 tablespoons unsalted butter

Spicy Ginger Broth with Pork Meatballs and Bok Choy SERVES 4

AROMATICS, SUCH AS LEMONGRASS and ginger, give this broth heft and depth. If you make the broth and the meatballs in advance, the soup itself comes together easily. For a vegetarian variation, use vegetable stock and substitute tofu for the meatballs.

For the broth, in a medium saucepan heat the olive oil over medium heat and add the shallot, garlic, and ginger; sauté until they begin to color lightly. Add the jalapeño, lemongrass, turmeric, coriander seed, and white peppercorns, and stir to combine. Cook until the spices are lightly toasted and fragrant, about 1 minute. Add the stock and bring to a boil. Reduce the heat and simmer for 30 minutes. Remove from the heat and let the broth sit at room temperature for 1 hour. Strain through a fine-mesh strainer (discard solids) and refrigerate until ready to use.

For the meatballs, in a medium sauté pan heat the canola oil over medium heat. Add the red onion and garlic and cook until softened. Remove from the heat and let cool completely. In a large bowl, combine the ground pork with the egg, soy sauce, honey, and cooked onion and garlic. Add the breadcrumbs, season with salt and pepper, and mix together with your hands or a spoon until fully incorporated. Refrigerate the mixture for 1 hour.

Preheat the oven to 350°F.

Shape the pork mixture into 1-ounce balls and place them on a baking sheet. Bake for 25 minutes. Remove from the oven and set aside or refrigerate until ready to assemble the soup.

For the soup, starting at the leafy end of the baby bok choy, slice each head into thin strips until you reach the root end. Cut off and discard the last bit of the root. In a large saucepan or a Dutch oven, heat the canola oil over medium heat and add the sliced bok choy, carrots, and celery. Cook for about 1 minute. Stir in the grated ginger and continue cooking for 1 minute. Add the prepared broth and simmer for 5 minutes.

Add the meatballs and return the broth to a simmer. Simmer until the meatballs are heated through, 7 to 10 minutes. Stir in the cooked rice and sambal and simmer for 1 to 2 minutes, then remove from the heat. Season with salt to taste. To serve, ladle the soup into serving bowls and top with the scallions and sesame seeds.

BROTH

1 tablespoon extra-virgin olive oil

1 shallot, chopped

2 cloves garlic, chopped

1 thumb-size piece of ginger, thinly sliced

1 small jalapeño pepper, thinly sliced

One 3-inch piece lemongrass, crushed

¼ teaspoon ground turmeric

1 teaspoon coriander seed

½ teaspoon whole white peppercorns

4 cups chicken stock

MEATBALLS

1 tablespoon canola oil

1 small red onion, minced

2 cloves garlic, minced

8 ounces ground pork

1 large egg, beaten

1 tablespoon soy sauce

1 tablespoon honey

¾ cup panko breadcrumbs

Kosher salt and freshly ground black pepper

SOUP

3 heads baby bok choy

2 tablespoons canola oil

2 medium carrots, cut into thin strips

2 ribs celery, thinly sliced

1 tablespoon grated fresh ginger

1 cup cooked jasmine rice

2 tablespoons sambal sauce

Kosher salt

4 scallions, thinly sliced

1 tablespoon toasted sesame seeds

Chicken, Vegetable, and Orzo Soup SERVES 4 TO 6

1 pound boneless, skinless
   chicken thighs

2 tablespoons canola oil, plus
   more for brushing

1 teaspoon celery salt

Freshly ground black pepper

2 tablespoons kosher salt,
   plus more to taste

1 cup orzo pasta

1 small bulb fennel, diced
   (about 1 cup)

2 to 3 medium carrots, diced
   (about 1 cup)

3 to 4 ribs celery, diced
   (about 1 cup)

2 leeks, white parts diced
   (about 1 cup)

2 tablespoons chopped garlic

6 cups chicken stock

3 cups baby spinach leaves

EVERYONE SHOULD HAVE a go-to chicken soup recipe. Some version of chicken soup is found in almost every culture, with recipes as ancient as our ability to boil water. My version is flexible: once you learn the basics, you can swap out the vegetables depending on what you have on hand. I use orzo because it holds up well in broth and it's easy to eat with a spoon. This tastes better the day after it's made, especially with a few crumbled crackers on top.

Preheat the oven to 325°F.

Place the chicken thighs on a baking sheet lined with foil and brush generously with the canola oil. Season with the celery salt and a little pepper. Roast for 25 minutes. Remove and let cool. When the chicken is cool enough to handle, dice it into ½-inch pieces.

In a large pot, bring 4 cups water and the 2 tablespoons of salt to a boil. Add the orzo and cook for 10 minutes. Once the pasta is al dente, drain in a colander, then spread out on a baking sheet and let cool to room temperature. Add 1 teaspoon of the canola oil and stir to combine to keep the pasta from sticking.

In a large saucepan, heat the remaining 1 tablespoon plus 2 teaspoons canola oil over medium heat and add the fennel, carrots, and celery. Sauté until the vegetables begin to soften, 3 to 4 minutes. Add the leeks and garlic and stir to combine. Sauté until the leeks have wilted. Add the chicken stock and bring to a simmer. Simmer for 10 minutes. Add the chicken meat and orzo and return to a simmer, then simmer for 2 additional minutes. Season the soup with salt and pepper. Just before serving, add the baby spinach and cook until just wilted, 1 to 2 minutes. Serve hot.

White Bean and Ham Hock Stew SERVES 6 TO 8

WHEN I WAS GROWING UP, we had a woodstove in our house. On cold days, my mother would simmer ham hocks in a large pot over the stove, filling the house with the comforting aroma of ham broth. This soup was one of those pleasing and economical meals that could feed our family of seven, and I still enjoy making large batches of it to serve my family today. (It makes great leftovers, too.) Look for fully intact smoked ham hocks. You'll soak the hocks in cold water for about an hour before cooking to remove a bit of the salt, but keep in mind when seasoning this soup that the salt from the hocks still might make it salty enough. I serve this soup with toasted bread for dipping.

Place the ham hocks in a large pot and cover with cold water. Soak for 1 hour. Drain the ham hocks and return them to the pot. Add 1 gallon of water and place over high heat. Bring to a boil, then reduce the heat to a simmer. Cook until the hocks are falling apart, about 3 hours. Add more water as needed to keep the hocks covered by a few inches while simmering. Remove from the heat and let cool slightly. Use a slotted spoon to transfer the hocks to a cutting board. Strain the ham broth through a fine-mesh strainer into a large bowl and set aside. Once the hocks are cool enough to handle, pick the meat from the bones and roughly chop.

Drain the soaked beans and transfer to a large saucepan. Add cold water to cover and the 2 tablespoons salt and place over high heat. Bring to a boil, then remove from the heat. Drain the beans, discarding the liquid. Return the beans to the saucepan and add enough ham hock stock to cover the beans. Bring to a simmer over medium-high heat. Cook until the beans are tender, 25 to 35 minutes. Remove 1 cup of the cooked beans and 1½ cups of the broth and transfer those beans and broth to a blender; puree until smooth. Drain the remaining beans and set aside.

Clean out the saucepan, add the canola oil, and place over medium heat. Add the onion, celery, and carrots and sauté until the vegetables begin to soften, 3 to 4 minutes. Stir in the garlic and cook for 30 seconds. Add the drained beans, the bean puree, and 3 cups of the ham hock stock. Bring to a simmer and stir in the kale. Simmer for 20 additional minutes. Stir in the chopped meat and allow to warm through, 5 to 7 minutes. Taste and season lightly with salt and pepper, as needed. If the soup is a little thick, add more ham stock until it reaches your desired consistency.

2 pounds smoked ham hocks

2 cups dried great northern beans, soaked for 2 to 4 hours

2 tablespoons kosher salt, plus more to taste

3 tablespoons canola oil

2 small Spanish onions, diced (about 2 cups)

3 to 4 ribs celery, diced (about 1 cup)

2 to 3 medium carrots, diced (about 1 cup)

2 cloves garlic, chopped

1 bunch lacinato kale, stemmed and roughly chopped

Freshly ground black pepper

Lentil, Kale, and Tomato Soup SERVES 4 TO 6

3 tablespoons canola oil

1 small Spanish onion, diced (about 1 cup)

3 to 4 ribs celery, diced (about 1 cup)

¼ teaspoon ground turmeric

2 cups chopped curly kale

1 cup green lentils

6 cups vegetable stock

2 large beefsteak tomatoes, cored and diced, juices reserved

Kosher salt and freshly ground black pepper

¼ cup grated pecorino

1 teaspoon chili flakes

I LOVE THE EARTHY FLAVOR you get when pairing lentils with kale, but together they need a little brightness—hence the addition of tomatoes and cheese, which balances this simple soup. Aged pecorino, made with sheep's milk, is similar to Parmesan, but it has a more subtle flavor.

In a large saucepan, heat the canola oil over medium heat and add the onion and celery. Cook until the vegetables just begin to soften, 3 to 4 minutes. Stir in the turmeric and cook until fragrant, about 1 minute. Add the kale and lentils and stir to incorporate. Add the vegetable stock and raise the heat to medium-high to bring to a simmer. Simmer until the lentils are just cooked through, about 20 minutes. Add the tomatoes and their juices and continue to simmer for 10 additional minutes. Season to taste with salt and pepper.

To serve, spoon the soup into individual bowls and top with the pecorino and chili flakes.

Classic Caesar Salad with Garlic Confit Croutons SERVES 4 TO 6

CAESAR SALAD IS SAID to have been created by an Italian chef who moved to Mexico from California to avoid Prohibition. His name was Caesar Cardini. This salad has remained popular for decades because it hits a lot of the notes we love in a salad—salty, crunchy, with a bit of umami—and it's fairly simple to make. The dressing should be somewhat thick so that it sticks to the leaves, which I like to keep whole. Make sure your romaine is crisp and cold. I like warm croutons on this salad, so I make them right before serving.

In the bowl of a food processor fitted with the metal blade, combine the egg yolks, lemon juice, Dijon, capers, anchovies, Worcestershire, and garlic. Puree until well combined. Drizzle the canola and olive oils in a thin stream through the tube while processing. Season with salt and pepper and add the Parmesan. Pulse a few times until just mixed. Refrigerate the dressing for about 15 minutes. You may not need all the dressing, but you can refrigerate leftovers for up to 3 days.

Cut off the bottom of each romaine heart and separate all the leaves. In a large bowl, gently toss the leaves with the dressing by hand, being careful not to break the leaves. Make sure each leaf is coated and place the lettuce in a serving bowl. Top with croutons and season with freshly ground black pepper to taste.

2 egg yolks

¼ cup freshly squeezed lemon juice

1 tablespoon Dijon mustard

1 teaspoon capers, rinsed and drained

6 anchovy fillets packed in oil

1 tablespoon Worcestershire sauce

2 cloves garlic

½ cup canola oil

½ cup extra-virgin olive oil

Kosher salt and freshly ground black pepper

¼ cup finely grated Parmesan

3 romaine hearts, chilled

2 cups Garlic Confit Croutons (recipe follows)

Garlic Confit Croutons MAKES 2 CUPS

Preheat the oven to 300°F.

In a large bowl, toss the bread with the garlic confit to coat. Let sit for 10 minutes to allow the garlic and oil to soak in. Transfer to a baking sheet and bake for 10 minutes. Increase the heat to 375°F and toast for 5 additional minutes.

Remove from the oven and transfer the bread to a large bowl. Add the Parmesan, season with salt and pepper, and toss to combine. Serve warm or at room temperature.

2 cups cubed sourdough bread

¼ cup Garlic Confit (page 224)

¼ cup finely grated Parmesan

Kosher salt and freshly ground black pepper

Chef's Tip: I prefer white anchovies packed in oil, since they tend to have the mildest flavor. Anchovies packed in salt will also work, but be sure to rinse them and be cautious when seasoning the dressing.

Peach Salad with Ginger, Feta, and Watercress **SERVES 4**

One 2-inch piece ginger

¼ cup granulated sugar

¼ cup champagne vinegar

3 large ripe peaches

1 cup watercress leaves

½ cup crumbled feta

3 tablespoons extra-virgin
  olive oil

Kosher salt and freshly ground
  black pepper

½ teaspoon Aleppo pepper

YOU MUST HAVE PERFECTLY RIPE peaches for this recipe. Most grocery stores do not put out ripe fruit, so peaches usually need a couple of days to ripen after you purchase them. Buy them a few days in advance and store them in a sealed container at room temperature—they will ripen beautifully. Any other stone fruit will also work in this recipe—try it with nectarines. I usually remove the peach skin but you don't have to if you don't mind a bit of fuzz.

Rinse the ginger but leave the skin on. Slice into 5 or 6 pieces and place in a saucepan with the sugar and vinegar. Stir to combine. Bring to a boil, then reduce the heat to a simmer. Simmer gently for 5 minutes, then remove from the heat and allow to cool. Strain through a fine-mesh strainer into a bowl and discard the solids. Refrigerate ginger syrup until ready to use.

If you're keeping the peach skins, you can skip to pitting the peaches. If you're removing the peach skins, bring about 1 gallon of room temperature water to a boil in a large pot. Prepare an ice bath as on page 225. Use a paring knife to score the skin on the bottom of each peach. Carefully lower the peaches into the boiling water. After 10 seconds, remove them with a slotted spoon and transfer to the ice bath. (The peaches should not be cooked, but this makes them easier to peel.) Once the peaches are cool, peel them by starting at the scores in the skin. Pit the peaches and cut them into wedges. Place the peach wedges in a mixing bowl and add 2 tablespoons of the ginger syrup. Toss to combine.

Arrange the peach wedges on a platter. In the same bowl the peaches were in, toss the watercress with the feta, 2 tablespoons of the ginger syrup, and 2 tablespoons of the olive oil, and season with salt and pepper. Arrange the watercress on top of the peaches, drizzle the remaining 1 tablespoon olive oil on top, and sprinkle with Aleppo pepper before serving.

Simple Greens and Herb Salad SERVES 4

WHEN YOU ADD FRESH HERBS to salad greens, both gain brightness. I like this simple salad with a light champagne vinaigrette, which is easy to put together and will last in the fridge for about two weeks. (The dressing also makes a great marinade for chicken or pork.) Feel free to use a package of mixed greens or buy small amounts of your favorite greens at the market and make your own mix.

Place the greens and herbs in a large mixing bowl. Dress the salad with ¼ cup dressing and gently toss by hand to coat.

Taste and adjust dressing. Place in a serving bowl and garnish with apple slices and almonds.

4 cups mixed greens

1 cup mixed herb leaves, such as basil, dill, flat-leaf parsley, and mint

¼ cup Champagne Vinaigrette (recipe follows), plus more to taste

1 honeycrisp apple, cored and thinly sliced

½ cup sliced almonds, lightly toasted

Champagne Vinaigrette MAKES 1 CUP

Preheat the oven to 350°F (or use a toaster oven).

Brush the shallot with a little olive oil and place on a baking sheet. Roast for 10 minutes, then remove and let cool.

In a blender combine the shallot, thyme, Dijon, and vinegar and puree until smooth. While the blender is running, add ¼ cup plus 2 tablespoons of the olive oil through the tube in a thin stream while processing. Add 3 tablespoons cold water and then the remaining ¼ cup plus 2 tablespoons olive oil. Season to taste with salt and pepper. Refrigerate in an airtight container until ready to use.

1 small shallot, peeled

¾ cup extra-virgin olive oil, plus more for brushing shallot

2 teaspoons fresh thyme leaves

2 tablespoons Dijon mustard

¼ cup champagne vinegar

Kosher salt and freshly ground black pepper

Cucumber and Fennel Salad   SERVES 4

2 English cucumbers, a few
   strips of skin peeled off
   lengthwise

½ cup crème fraîche

1 teaspoon finely grated lemon
   zest

3 tablespoons freshly squeezed
   lemon juice

Kosher salt and freshly ground
   black pepper

1 small bulb fennel, cored and
   thinly sliced on a mandolin

5 medium mint leaves

½ cup arugula

1 large breakfast radish, thinly
   sliced

¼ cup toasted pistachios,
   crushed

THIS SIMPLE SALAD is full of bright flavors and works as a side dish or a starter. English cucumbers work best (and they're pretty consistently available)—and I like to leave a little peel on to add color. If you don't have mint, try tarragon or dill.

Slice the cucumbers in half lengthwise and scoop out and discard the seeds. Slice each half into thin slices on a slight angle.

In a medium bowl, combine the crème fraîche with the lemon zest and juice, and season with salt and pepper. Add the fennel and cucumber and fold together with the crème fraîche. On a cutting board, layer the mint leaves on top of one another and cut into thin strips; stir into the cucumbers and fennel. Season with more salt and pepper to taste.

To serve, place the arugula in the bottom of a serving bowl and spoon the cucumber mixture on top. Garnish with radish and pistachio. Serve slightly chilled.

Snap Pea and Radish Salad SERVES 4 TO 6

THIS SALAD TAKES a little bit of effort, but the results are worth it. Look for watermelon radishes, as they add color. And if you like a little heat, try adding a few pickled Fresno peppers (see page 43).

Bring a medium saucepan of salted water to a boil and prepare an ice bath as on page 225. Blanch the snap peas for 30 seconds. Use a slotted spoon to remove them from the pot and transfer to the ice bath. Drain and transfer to a towel to dry. Slice the peas at an angle into thin strips and set aside.

Meanwhile, place the mustard seeds in a dry sauté pan and set over low heat. Toast the seeds, moving the pan constantly so the seeds don't burn. Once they are fragrant, remove from the heat and let cool. Transfer to a spice grinder and grind finely.

In a large bowl, combine the crème fraîche, sour cream, and lemon zest and juice. Season with salt and pepper to taste.

Add the snap peas and mint to the bowl and toss to combine. Season with salt and pepper. Transfer to a serving dish and top with the sliced radishes. Garnish with toasted mustard seeds and chives before serving.

Kosher salt

2½ cups snap peas, strings removed

1 tablespoon yellow mustard seed

1 tablespoon black mustard seed

¼ cup crème fraîche

2 tablespoons sour cream

Finely grated zest and juice of 1 lemon

Freshly ground black pepper

12 mint leaves, julienned

2 radishes, thinly sliced

1 tablespoon minced fresh chives

Chef's Tip: To remove the string that runs down the length of each snap pea pod, use a paring knife to clip the stem and pull it down along the seam; discard the stem and string.

Pickled Beets with Creamy Goat Cheese and Toasted Almonds SERVES 4

4 to 5 small red beets (golf ball–size) with tops

¼ cup kosher salt, plus more to taste

2 cups white wine vinegar

1 cup granulated sugar

1 teaspoon fennel seed

1 teaspoon mustard seed

1 teaspoon whole black peppercorns

1 teaspoon celery seed

½ teaspoon coriander seed

2 sprigs rosemary (optional)

2 ounces soft goat cheese, room temperature

2 ounces crème fraîche

¼ cup heavy cream

2 teaspoons extra-virgin olive oil

1 teaspoon freshly squeezed lemon juice

Freshly ground black pepper

¾ cup raw unsalted almonds, toasted and crushed

1 tablespoon minced fresh chives (optional)

Chef's Tip: Once the beets are cooked and in the pickling liquid in the jar, they will keep in the refrigerator for up to 3 weeks.

AT HOME, I DON'T EAT much goat cheese unless it's on this salad. Seek out a nice, pungent cheese with no rind to complement the pickled beets. For the pickling liquid, I like to wrap the spices in a coffee filter or cheesecloth tied tightly with kitchen twine so that they're easy to remove and discard. Reserve the beet tops to sauté as you would the greens on page 150. And be sure to wear gloves while cleaning beets. Use a cake tester to test them for doneness—it should pierce them easily.

Remove the tops from the beets and rinse under cold water to remove any dirt. Place them in a large pot and add 1 gallon cold water, the ¼ cup salt, the vinegar, and the sugar. Place the fennel seed, mustard seed, peppercorns, celery seed, coriander seed, and rosemary, if using, in a coffee filter or cheesecloth and tie tightly with twine. Add to the pot. Bring the pickling liquid to a simmer and simmer until the beets are cooked through and can be easily pierced with a cake tester, 25 to 35 minutes. Remove from the heat and allow the beets to cool in the liquid.

When the beets are cool enough to handle, remove from the liquid and use a paper towel to rub off the skins; they should come off easily. Use a paring knife to trim the stem ends and remove any stubborn bits of peel. Cut the beets into wedges and place in a large jar. Strain the pickling liquid over the beets, seal the jar with the lid, and refrigerate until cold.

When ready to compose the salad, place the goat cheese in a food processor fitted with the metal blade and pulse to break into small chunks. Add the crème fraîche and cream and pulse until just combined; do not overmix or the cream will begin to separate from the cheese. Season with salt.

To serve, spread the goat cheese mixture on a serving plate. Drain the beets and transfer to a large bowl. Toss with the olive oil and lemon juice and season with salt and pepper. Arrange the beets on top of the goat cheese and top with the toasted almonds and chives, if using.

Farro Salad with Tomatoes, Arugula, and Ricotta Salata SERVES 4

FARRO IS A FLAVORFUL GRAIN that offers a firm bite—I like it because it stands up well even in cold salads. You can also use it in soups or cook it like a risotto. Use restraint when seasoning this salad as the ricotta salata is already naturally salty.

In a medium saucepan, combine the farro, 5 cups water, the vinegar, and the 2 tablespoons salt and place over medium heat. Bring to a simmer and continue simmering until the farro is tender, about 30 minutes. Drain well and spread on a baking sheet to cool slightly, then transfer to a mixing bowl and refrigerate for 30 minutes.

When ready to serve, remove the bowl from the refrigerator and add the arugula and pesto; season with salt and pepper. Stir to coat. To serve, transfer to a serving dish and top with the tomatoes and ricotta salata.

1 cup farro

2 tablespoons cider vinegar

2 tablespoons kosher salt, plus more to taste

2 cups baby arugula leaves

¼ cup Basil Pesto (page 167)

Freshly ground black pepper

2 pints medley cherry tomatoes, halved or quartered

¼ cup grated ricotta salata

Couscous Salad with Herb Vinaigrette SERVES 4

1½ cups vegetable stock

Kosher salt

1 cup Israeli couscous

1 Roasted Red Pepper (page 224)

4 stalks broccoli rabe, blanched

1 cup medley cherry tomatoes, quartered

1 cup Cooked Chickpeas (page 230)

Freshly ground black pepper

About ½ cup Herb Vinaigrette (recipe follows)

½ cucumber, diced

½ cup crumbled feta

LET'S CALL THIS the no-rules salad. There are no rules to the vegetables you should use or how much vinaigrette you need. You can serve it warm or cold. Really, the only restrictions are that you need to dress the vegetables with the vinaigrette before adding the couscous (it keeps the couscous from getting soggy), and if you're making it ahead, don't dress until you're ready to serve it. Otherwise, add, subtract, and make this salad your own.

In a medium saucepan, bring the vegetable stock to a boil and add a pinch of salt. Stir in the couscous and simmer for 1 minute, then remove the pan from the heat. Cover with a tight-fitting lid and let stand for 15 minutes. Remove the lid and drain off any excess liquid. Spread the couscous on a baking sheet. With a fork, separate and fluff the pieces. Let cool.

Dice the roasted bell pepper. Chop the broccoli rabe into small pieces. Place both in a mixing bowl along with the tomatoes and chickpeas and season with salt and pepper. Add ½ cup of the vinaigrette and toss to combine. Add the couscous and toss to combine. Taste and add more vinaigrette, if needed. Transfer to a serving bowl and top with the cucumber and feta.

Herb Vinaigrette MAKES ABOUT 1¼ CUPS

¾ cup extra-virgin olive oil

½ cup flat-leaf parsley leaves

½ cup basil, cilantro, and mint leaves

3 tablespoons apple cider vinegar

2 tablespoons honey

1 teaspoon Dijon mustard

Kosher salt and freshly ground black pepper

In a jar or other container, combine the olive oil, herbs, vinegar, honey, and mustard. Use an immersion blender to puree and combine. Season with salt and pepper. Seal tightly and refrigerate until ready to use.

Iceberg, Cucumber, and Carrot Salad with Blue Cheese SERVES 4

THIS IS MY VERSION of a classic wedge salad—I love the crunchy sweetness of iceberg lettuce, and a good salad allows it to shine. The blue cheese is key, so be sure to find a quality brand—you want something that crumbles and is not too creamy. This salad would not be mad if you added a handful of lardons.

In a countertop deep fryer or a heavy-bottomed pot or Dutch oven, heat the canola oil to 350°F. Add the wonton strips and fry until golden brown. Transfer to a paper towel–lined plate and season with salt and pepper.

In a food processor fitted with the metal blade, combine ¾ cup of the blue cheese with the sour cream and buttermilk. Pulse until the mixture is combined but still a little chunky. Season with a small amount of black pepper and refrigerate until ready to serve.

Remove the core from the iceberg and cut the head of lettuce in half. Arrange flat-side down and slice into thin strips. Place in a mixing bowl. Peel the cucumber and carrot. Slice the cucumber in half lengthwise and scoop out the seeds. Cut it in half lengthwise again, then cut into thin pieces. Slice the carrot into thin rounds then slice the thin rounds into strips. Add the cucumber and carrot to the bowl with the iceberg.

Pour the blue cheese dressing over the salad and toss to combine. Transfer to a serving bowl and top with the remaining ¼ cup blue cheese, sliced scallions, and crispy wontons.

2 cups canola oil

6 wonton wrappers, cut into thin strips

Kosher salt and freshly ground black pepper

1 cup crumbled blue cheese

¼ cup sour cream

¼ cup buttermilk

1 head iceberg lettuce

1 English cucumber

1 large carrot

2 scallions, green parts only, thinly sliced

Chef's Tip: Bacon lardons are ¼-inch-thick slices of bacon that have been cooked until crispy. Add them to this salad or to soups, stews, or potato dishes to add texture and flavor.

Cauliflower, Apple, and Pomegranate Salad

SERVES 4

1 small head cauliflower, cut into small florets

¼ cup extra-virgin olive oil

Kosher salt and freshly ground black pepper

1 head romaine lettuce

1 large honeycrisp apple

½ cup pomegranate seeds

½ cup Cider Shallot Vinaigrette (recipe follows)

THIS SALAD SPEAKS TO ME of fall—it's crunchy, sweet, and tart. I also like the color, thanks to the pomegranate seeds—these are easy to find in the produce section of most grocery stores—and the apples, which I usually use with the skin intact to add more crunch.

Preheat the oven to 400°F.

Place the cauliflower florets on a baking sheet and toss with the olive oil. Season with salt and pepper. Roast until the florets are softened and beginning to color around the edges, about 20 minutes. Remove from the oven and allow to cool to room temperature. Transfer to a large mixing bowl.

Cut the root end from the lettuce and separate the leaves. Slice the large leaves in half both lengthwise and crosswise. Add to the bowl with the cauliflower. Core the apple and dice into ½-inch pieces. Add those to the mixing bowl with ¼ cup pomegranate seeds. Add the vinaigrette and season with salt and pepper. Toss to combine. Transfer the salad to a serving bowl and sprinkle the remaining ¼ cup pomegranate seeds on top.

Cider Shallot Vinaigrette

MAKES ABOUT 1 CUP

1 small shallot, peeled

¼ cup canola oil

2 teaspoons Dijon mustard

1 teaspoon grated fresh ginger

¼ cup apple cider

3 tablespoons apple cider vinegar

¼ cup extra-virgin olive oil

Kosher salt and freshly ground black pepper

Preheat the oven to 350°F (or use a toaster oven).

Brush the shallot with a little of the canola oil and roast for 12 minutes. Remove and let sit until cool enough to handle. Place the shallot in a blender with the mustard, ginger, cider, and vinegar. Blend until smooth, then add the remaining canola oil and the olive oil in a thin stream through the tube while processing. Season with salt and pepper to taste. Refrigerate in an airtight container until ready to use. The vinaigrette can be refrigerated for up to 2 weeks.

Egg and Potato Salad with Bacon and Sunflower Seeds SERVES 4

DISHES LIKE THIS HUMBLE EGG and potato salad are handed down through generations because they are reliably good and easy to prepare. This version is a throwback to a salad that my mom might have made. I like to use small medley potatoes in a mix of colors, but you can substitute any potatoes you have on hand. Potatoes like salt, so be sure to salt the water really well before cooking. Serve this with a few hunks of crusty bread or crackers.

Place the eggs in a medium saucepan with cold water to cover them by a few inches. Place over high heat and bring to a rolling boil. Boil for 30 seconds, then remove from the heat and cover with a tight-fitting lid. Let the eggs sit for 12 minutes, then drain the water. Fill the saucepan with ice water and let the eggs sit for about 20 minutes, or until the eggs are completely chilled. Shell the eggs.

Preheat the oven to 375°F.

Place the bacon strips on a baking sheet and bake until very crisp, 15 to 20 minutes. Remove and let cool. Chop or crumble and set aside.

Place the potatoes in a medium saucepan and add cold water to cover. Salt generously. Bring to a simmer over medium-high heat. Cook until the potatoes are tender but not falling apart, about 8 minutes. Drain and spread on a baking sheet to cool to room temperature.

In a large mixing bowl, combine the garlic confit, lemon juice, and paprika. Use a fork to mash them into a paste. Stir in the mayonnaise and Dijon. Season with salt and pepper to taste.

Once the potatoes are completely cooled, add them to the bowl with the mayonnaise mixture and toss to coat. Add more salt if needed. Cut each egg into 4 wedges and place on top of the potatoes. Top the salad with the bacon, scallion greens, sunflower seeds, and parsley and season to taste with black pepper.

3 large eggs

4 thick-cut strips bacon

1 pound medley potatoes, quartered

Kosher salt

2 teaspoons Garlic Confit (page 224)

1 tablespoon freshly squeezed lemon juice

¼ teaspoon paprika

¼ cup mayonnaise

1 tablespoon plus 1½ teaspoons Dijon mustard

Freshly ground black pepper

4 scallions, green parts only, thinly sliced on an angle

2 tablespoons sunflower seeds

2 tablespoons chopped flat-leaf parsley leaves

Chapter 4
Small Bites and Starters

One of my favorite rituals when all three of my kids are under the same roof or when we get together with friends is to put out a platter or two of tasty snacks and catch up while we graze. Meals don't have to be traditional; they are just meant to bring people together. Good food tends to do that. Snacks might seem like something you could pull from a bag or gather from the store, but it's much more of an occasion when you whip something up from scratch. These recipes are all easy and approachable. Don't be afraid of small substitutions to accommodate your tastes or your guests' preferences—these are all recipes that you can, and should, make your own.

Smoked Salmon and Caviar on Rye Crackers

MAKES 24 PIECES

NOW THAT CAVIAR IS widely available and accessible, you can (and should) enjoy it on elegant occasions, or just on a Tuesday. This easy snack feels like something my parents might have put out at a holiday party in the 1970s—but since all you have to do is shop and assemble, it can come out any time of year. Remember: Not all fish eggs are caviar, so look for high-quality sturgeon caviar, preferably osetra. I like to make my own smoked salmon or lox (you can find those recipes in *The Row 34 Cookbook*) but it's just as easy to buy. A little fresh dill on top makes this snack feel extra-fancy.

Place a small dollop of sour cream on each cracker. Cut the smoked salmon into small pieces and arrange them on the crackers next to and on top of the sour cream. Place a little caviar on top of each portion of smoked salmon. Sprinkle with lemon zest and garnish each with dill.

¼ cup sour cream

24 rye crackers

4 ounces sliced smoked salmon, cold

1 ounce caviar

Finely grated zest of 1 lemon

Fresh dill sprigs, cut into ½-inch lengths

Grilled Shrimp with Papaya and Avocado

SERVES 4 AS AN APPETIZER

1 pound (size U21/25) shrimp, peeled and deveined

¼ cup extra-virgin olive oil

1 tablespoon chopped garlic

¼ cup plus 2 tablespoons freshly squeezed lime juice

1 teaspoon paprika

Kosher salt and freshly ground black pepper

2 medium papayas, peeled, seeded, and cut into chunks (see Chef's Tip)

1 orange, supremed (see Chef's Tip on page 122), juices reserved

2 avocados

1 teaspoon Aleppo pepper

_____

Chef's Tip: To cut a papaya into chunks, cut the ends off the fruit and use a vegetable peeler to peel off the skin. Cut the papaya in half lengthwise and scoop out the seeds. Arrange the pieces flat-side down on a cutting board and cut into strips, then cut the strips into chunks.

WHEN GRILLING SHRIMP, I like larger pieces—look for U21/25 on the label, which means there will be 21 to 25 shrimp per pound. The fruit should be optimally ripe. Buy the papaya and avocado a few days in advance and let them ripen in a sealed container at room temperature.

In a large bowl, combine the shrimp with 2 tablespoons of the olive oil, the garlic, 2 tablespoons of the lime juice, and the paprika. Season with salt and pepper and stir to combine. Refrigerate for at least 1 hour and up to 3 hours (but no more).

Preheat a grill to medium-high and clean the grates.

Drain excess marinade from the bowl and place the shrimp on the grill grates. Grill the shrimp until cooked through and slightly charred, 2 to 3 minutes per side. Remove and set aside. (The shrimp can be chilled or used warm.)

Place the papaya in a medium bowl and add the orange segments and reserved juice. Season with a little salt.

Split the avocados and remove the pits. Scoop the flesh into another medium bowl and add the remaining ¼ cup lime juice. Mash the avocado with a fork to combine. Season with salt and pepper.

Transfer the avocado to a serving dish. Spoon the papaya mixture over the top. Arrange the shrimp over the papaya and drizzle with the remaining 2 tablespoons olive oil. Finish with the Aleppo pepper and serve.

Toasted Sourdough with Walnut Butter and Radish Salad SERVES 4

WALNUT BUTTER IS ONE OF those easy-to-make, tasty staples that you will use for the rest of your life. It is great on toast, melted over roasted vegetables, added to pasta, or—my favorite—dabbed on French toast. Freeze it to extend its life.

Preheat the oven to 375°F.

Melt the butter in a sauté pan over medium heat until it begins to brown lightly. Add the walnuts and stir to coat. Cook, stirring occasionally, until the walnuts begin to color, 3 to 4 minutes. Remove from the heat and transfer to the bowl of a food processor fitted with the metal blade. Season with salt and pepper, then process until smooth. It's okay if there are still a few lumps. Scrape into a storage container and let sit at room temperature.

Place the baguette slices on a baking sheet and toast for 3 to 4 minutes. Remove from the oven and spread each with walnut butter. Toast for 5 additional minutes. Remove and set aside.

Using a mandolin or very sharp knife, slice the radishes into thin rounds. Place in a mixing bowl with the baby watercress. Add the olive oil and lemon juice and toss to combine. To serve, top each slice of buttered toast with radish salad and cut each slice into 3 equal pieces. Arrange on a platter and finish each piece with sea salt.

2 sticks (16 tablespoons) unsalted butter

1 cup walnuts

Kosher salt and freshly ground black pepper

4 slices sourdough bread

6 to 8 radishes

1 cup baby watercress or arugula leaves

2 tablespoons extra-virgin olive oil

1 teaspoon freshly squeezed lemon juice

1 tablespoon sea salt

Chef's Tip: You can extend the shelf life of nuts by keeping them in a well-sealed container in the freezer.

Lobster Rangoon with Ponzu Sauce

MAKES 24 PIECES

6 ounces cooked lobster meat, chopped

4 ounces cream cheese, softened

1 tablespoon grated fresh ginger

½ teaspoon grated garlic

1 teaspoon finely grated orange zest

2 scallions, very thinly sliced, green and white parts separated (use whites in Ponzu Sauce)

Kosher salt and freshly ground black pepper

1 egg white

1 tablespoon cornstarch

Twenty-four 3 by 3–inch wonton wrappers

4 cups canola oil

¾ cup Ponzu Sauce (recipe follows)

FOR THE PONZU SAUCE

¼ cup soy sauce

3 tablespoons freshly squeezed lime juice

2 tablespoons rice wine vinegar

¼ cup orange juice

1 teaspoon grated fresh ginger

1 clove garlic, grated

Sliced scallion whites from above

1 tablespoon sriracha (optional)

WHILE THERE'S NO CONFIRMED origin story for crab Rangoon—luscious fried dumplings filled with crab—many attribute the recipe to a cook working at the famous Trader Vic's restaurant in San Francisco in the 1950s. It's highly unlikely that the recipe is Chinese in origin, but it's certainly associated with great Chinese American takeout. I make my version with lobster, but these can also be made with crab or shrimp. After the pieces are fried, let them cool for a minute before eating so you don't get a mouthful of cream cheese lava.

Pat the lobster meat dry. In a large bowl, combine the lobster, cream cheese, ginger, garlic, orange zest, and sliced scallion greens and stir to combine. Season with salt and pepper. (Go easy on the salt as the ponzu sauce is naturally salty.)

Line a baking sheet with parchment paper. In a small bowl, whisk together the egg white and cornstarch. Arrange 4 of the wonton wrappers on the parchment paper. Brush the sides of each wrapper with the egg white mixture. Place about 1 tablespoon of filling in the center of each wrapper. Carefully bring two of the four corners of a wrapper together and firmly pinch the seams so the filling is surrounded by the wrapper with no gaps. Pinch the remaining two corners together, creating a purse-like shape. Place the folded wontons on a tray and cover with a damp towel. Repeat with the remaining wrappers and filling.

In a countertop deep fryer or heavy-bottomed pot or Dutch oven, heat the canola oil to 350°F. Use a slotted spoon to drop a few prepared wontons into the oil. Move them around with the spoon, turning them a few times, so that they cook evenly. Fry until golden brown, 2 to 3 minutes total. Transfer to a paper towel–lined plate to drain. Repeat with the remaining wontons. Transfer to a serving platter and serve with ponzu sauce for dipping.

Ponzu Sauce **MAKES ABOUT ¾ CUP**

Place all ingredients in a lidded jar or container and cover tightly. Shake well to combine. Refrigerate until ready to serve. Shake again before serving.

Anchovy Toast with Lemon and Pickled Jalapeños SERVES 4

IF YOU'RE NEW TO ANCHOVIES, get on board—there are so many kinds out there and they pack a punch of flavor. I prefer using white anchovies packed in oil for this dish. The tomato sauce makes a great base for these toasts, but you could also use mashed avocado or crème fraîche. If you like pickled jalapeños, the recipe here makes a little more than you'll need and they're excellent in salads or on tacos. Be sure to assemble these toasts right before serving as the whole combination tastes better when the bread is still warm.

Preheat the oven to 350°F.

Brush the sliced ciabatta with the olive oil and toast in the oven for 8 minutes. Once they are cool enough to handle, spread tomato sauce on each slice and return to the oven for 5 minutes.

Remove the bread from the oven. Fold each anchovy fillet in half and place 2 or 3 fillets on each slice of toast. Arrange a few pickled jalapeños on top of or next to the anchovy fillets and garnish each toast with lemon zest and chopped parsley. Drizzle with lemon juice and sprinkle with sea salt.

1 loaf ciabatta bread, sliced into 16 pieces

½ cup extra-virgin olive oil

1 cup Tomato Sauce (page 226)

Two 4-ounce cans white anchovy fillets packed in oil (see Chef's Tip on page 71)

About ¼ cup Pickled Jalapeño Peppers (recipe follows)

Finely grated zest and juice of 1 lemon

3 tablespoons roughly chopped flat-leaf parsley leaves

Sea salt

Pickled Jalapeño Peppers

MAKES ABOUT ½ CUP

Use a mandolin to slice the jalapeños into thin rounds. Let some of the seeds fall away but keep a few mixed in with the slices. Place the slices and any seeds into a lidded glass jar along with the salt.

In a small saucepan, combine the vinegar, sugar, and garlic and bring to a boil. Carefully pour the hot liquid into the jar. It should cover the jalapeños. Allow to cool to room temperature, stirring occasionally. Once cool, cover with the lid and refrigerate. Pickled jalapeños will last for about 2 weeks in the refrigerator.

2 medium jalapeño peppers

1½ teaspoons kosher salt

½ cup rice wine vinegar

⅓ cup granulated sugar

1 clove garlic

Chef's Tip: To make pickled shallots, replace the jalapeños with 2 small shallots.

Fried Scallion Bread with Marinated Sun-Dried Tomatoes, Brie, and Kalamata Olives SERVES 4 AS AN APPETIZER

1½ cups all-purpose flour

½ cup whole wheat flour

2 teaspoons baking powder

2 teaspoons kosher salt

1 teaspoon freshly ground black pepper

2 scallions, green parts only, thinly sliced

1 tablespoon honey

2 tablespoons extra-virgin olive oil

About ¼ cup canola oil

1 cup sun-dried tomatoes in oil, drained and chopped

8 ounces brie, cut into thin pieces

½ cup pitted Kalamata olives, halved

2 tablespoons fresh oregano leaves

THIS QUICK AND EASY recipe starts with a no-yeast dough that is pan-fried, topped, then baked. I give the dough a bit of bite with a dose of black pepper—it's my favorite part of the recipe. I prefer store-bought marinated sun-dried tomatoes that come in a jar. Keep a jar in your pantry for an easy addition to snacks. This dish also works well with thinly sliced fresh tomatoes.

In a large bowl, combine the flours, baking powder, salt, and pepper. Fold in the scallions. In a small bowl, combine the honey with ¾ cup warm water and stir until the honey is dissolved. Add the olive oil and stir to combine. Add the liquid to the dry ingredients and mix by hand until the dough forms a ball. Let the dough rest for 15 minutes, then remove from the bowl and cut into 4 equal portions.

On a lightly floured surface, shape each portion into a ball, then use a rolling pin to roll each piece into a circle about ¼ inch thick.

Preheat the oven to 400°F.

Place a medium sauté pan over medium heat and add the ¼ cup canola oil; heat until shimmering. Add one of the dough circles to the pan and fry on one side until lightly browned. Flip and repeat on the other side, about 1 minute per side. Transfer to a baking sheet, then repeat with the remaining dough, adding a little more oil if needed. Evenly divide the tomatoes, brie, and olives and layer them on top of each piece of fried bread. Bake until the brie is just softened, about 3 minutes. Remove and allow to cool slightly before cutting each bread into 4 to 6 pieces. Garnish with oregano before serving.

Mushroom Arancini with Roasted Red Pepper Pesto

MAKES ABOUT 32 PIECES

WHO DOESN'T LOVE rice and cheese? These bites make a great party dish since they can be prepared ahead and even frozen. Just thaw them in the refrigerator overnight and fry right before serving. If they feel a little wet while you're assembling them, roll them through some extra breadcrumbs before frying. The pesto can also be made ahead and frozen.

Place the mushrooms in the bowl of a food processor fitted with the metal blade and chop into small pieces.

In a Dutch oven or large sauté pan, heat the olive oil over medium heat. Add the onion and sauté until just softened, then add the mushrooms and continue to sauté until the moisture is cooked out of the mushrooms, 8 to 10 minutes. Add the rice and stir until thoroughly combined.

Add the stock ½ cup at a time, stirring well with a wooden spoon or rubber spatula between additions. Be sure to scrape the bottom and sides of the pan to make sure the rice is not sticking. The rice will continue to absorb the stock, so keep stirring frequently. Once all of the stock has been added, add the cream and continue to stir. When the liquid has mostly been absorbed and the rice has swelled and is tender, remove from the heat. Stir in the butter and Parmesan and season with salt and pepper to taste. Spread the rice on a baking sheet and refrigerate until completely cool.

Take 2 to 3 tablespoons of cooled rice in your hands and roll into a ball the size of a ping-pong ball. Place on a clean baking sheet. Repeat with the remaining rice mixture to make about 32 pieces. Once all arancini have been rolled, return the baking sheet to the refrigerator for 30 minutes.

Create a breading station by placing the flour, eggs, and breadcrumbs in three separate shallow bowls. Remove the rice balls from the refrigerator and, working quickly, dredge one in flour, then dip completely in the beaten eggs, letting any excess liquid drip off. Finally, dredge in the breadcrumbs. Repeat with each rice ball, placing them back on the baking sheet once breaded. Cover loosely with plastic wrap and return to the refrigerator.

(continues on next page)

8 ounces cremini mushrooms

3 tablespoons extra-virgin olive oil

1 small Spanish onion, minced

1 cup arborio rice

3 cups vegetable or chicken stock

1 cup heavy cream

3 tablespoons unsalted butter, softened

½ cup grated Parmesan

Kosher salt and freshly ground black pepper

1½ cups all-purpose flour

3 large eggs, beaten

4 cups panko breadcrumbs, pulsed in a food processor until fine

About 4 cups canola oil for frying

1 cup Roasted Red Pepper Pesto (recipe follows)

In a countertop deep fryer or a heavy-bottomed pot or Dutch oven, add enough canola oil to cover the arancini, about 4 cups, and bring to 350ºF. Place 3 or 4 cold rice balls in the oil and fry until golden brown. With a skimmer, remove to a paper towel–lined plate to drain. Season with salt and pepper. Continue frying the rice balls in batches. Serve with the pesto on the side.

Roasted Red Pepper Pesto

MAKES ABOUT 1 CUP

¼ cup extra-virgin olive oil

1 Roasted Red Pepper (page 224) plus 2 tablespoons reserved roasting liquid, or 1 jarred roasted red pepper, drained, plus 2 tablespoons of the liquid from the jar

2 tablespoons pine nuts, toasted

½ cup grated Parmesan

12 large basil leaves

1 clove garlic

Kosher salt and freshly ground black pepper

In a blender or the bowl of a food processor fitted with the metal blade, combine the olive oil, red pepper and liquid, pine nuts, Parmesan, basil leaves, and garlic. Puree until smooth. Season with salt and pepper to taste. Refrigerate until ready to serve, or portion into small batches in airtight containers and freeze.

Marinated Tomatoes with Burrata and Prosciutto

SERVES 4 AS AN APPETIZER

THIS IS SUCH AN ICONIC tomato dish, and for good reason—the flavors combine into a sweet, salty, tangy combination. I have a romantic vision in my head of going to a farmer's market to get the best tomatoes and freshest burrata and then heading to an Italian deli to find freshly sliced prosciutto for this salad. That rarely happens, but if you have a good farmer's market near you, stop by in late summer when the tomatoes are at their peak. Perfect tomatoes, super-fresh basil, and high-quality olive oil take this dish over the top. Share a whole platter of it with family and friends while sitting outside drinking rosé.

Preheat the oven to 400°F.

Remove the cores from the heirloom and beefsteak tomatoes. Slice each in half lengthwise and arrange flat-side down on a cutting board. Slice the tomatoes in half lengthwise again, then cut into thin wedges. Place the cut tomatoes in a bowl along with the cherry tomatoes and add the balsamic vinegar and the ¼ cup olive oil. Take half of the basil leaves and tear into pieces. Add them to the tomato mix. Toss gently so the tomatoes don't fall apart.

Brush each slice of sourdough lightly with olive oil, place on a baking sheet, and toast in the oven for 10 minutes. Cut each slice into 2 or 3 pieces.

Place the burrata in the middle of a wide, shallow bowl and spoon the tomato mixture around it. Season well with salt and pepper, and add the Aleppo pepper. Garnish with the remaining basil leaves. Place the prosciutto and bread on separate plates. Cut the burrata open and encourage everyone to smear a little of the burrata on a slice of bread, spoon some of the tomatoes and dressing over it, and tear off a piece of prosciutto to set on top.

1 large heirloom tomato

1 beefsteak tomato

½ cup medley cherry tomatoes, halved

¼ cup balsamic vinegar

¼ cup extra-virgin olive oil, plus more for brushing

12 to 15 fresh basil leaves

4 slices sourdough bread

One 8-ounce ball burrata

Sea salt

Freshly ground black pepper

½ teaspoon Aleppo pepper

8 slices prosciutto

Pork Dumplings with Shiitake Mushrooms and Spicy Garlic Sauce MAKES 25 PIECES

THIS IS A GREAT RECIPE to make with the whole family. I like to get the kids involved in folding the dumplings. I recommend using a nonstick sauté pan with a fitted lid for cooking the dumplings. You'll need to cook them in batches. If you'd like to work ahead, they freeze pretty well once formed; just cook them right from the freezer.

For the filling, in a large sauté pan, heat the canola oil over medium heat and add the onion. Cook until it begins to color lightly, 2 to 3 minutes. Add the cabbage, garlic, ginger, and the whites of scallions, and sauté until the cabbage softens, about 5 minutes. Remove from the heat and let cool. In a large bowl, combine the ground pork with the cooled cabbage mixture and stir in the soy sauce, salt, and pepper. Cover and refrigerate for 1 hour.

For the dumplings, line a baking sheet with parchment paper. In a small bowl, whisk the egg white and cornstarch. Arrange 4 or 5 dumpling wrappers on a work surface and brush the edges very lightly with the egg wash. (Too much will make them hard to seal.) Place about 1 tablespoon of filling in the center of each wrapper and pick up a dumpling. Fold into a semicircle and pinch the edges together at the center of the wrapper seam, then work your way around the seam, pinching the wrapper together firmly to push out any air as you seal. Place the dumpling on the parchment paper and repeat until all are filled and sealed. Cover loosely with plastic wrap and refrigerate until ready to assemble, or freeze if making ahead.

To cook the dumplings, in a nonstick sauté pan with a lid (the pan should be large enough to hold half of the dumplings in a single layer without overcrowding), heat ½ cup of the canola oil over medium-high heat. Add the shiitakes and sauté until crisp. Transfer to a paper towel–lined plate and season with salt. In the same pan over medium-high, heat 1 tablespoon of the remaining oil. Add half of the dumplings. Sear the dumplings on one side and turn when they begin to brown. Immediately add ¼ cup water and cover with the lid. Allow the dumplings to steam for 3 minutes, then remove the pan from the heat. Transfer the cooked dumplings to a plate and repeat with the remaining 1 tablespoon oil and the dumplings.

To serve, place the dumplings in a serving bowl and drizzle with spicy garlic sauce. Top with the crisp shiitakes and scallion greens.

FILLING

2 tablespoons canola oil

1 small Spanish onion, minced

2 large leaves Napa cabbage, stemmed and thinly sliced

1 teaspoon grated garlic

1 teaspoon grated fresh ginger

4 scallions, thinly sliced, white and green parts separated

8 ounces ground pork

2 tablespoons soy sauce

1 teaspoon salt

¼ teaspoon freshly ground black pepper

DUMPLINGS

1 large egg white

1 tablespoon cornstarch

Twenty-five 3-inch round dumpling wrappers

SERVING

½ cup plus 2 tablespoons canola oil

8 ounces shiitake mushrooms, stemmed and thinly sliced

Kosher salt

½ cup Spicy Garlic Sauce (recipe follows)

Spicy Garlic Sauce MAKES ABOUT ½ CUP

2 teaspoons Garlic Confit (page 224)

¼ cup soy sauce

2 tablespoons sambal sauce

1 tablespoon sriracha

2 tablespoons rice wine vinegar

1 tablespoon sesame seeds, toasted

1 tablespoon grated fresh ginger

1 tablespoon toasted sesame oil

2 tablespoons honey

In a medium bowl, whisk together all of the ingredients until combined.

Roasted Eggplant on Grilled Bread

SERVES 4 AS AN APPETIZER

THIS IS THE ULTIMATE summer appetizer. I like to add the flavorful Middle Eastern spice mix za'atar. I toast it before combining it with the eggplant, which makes the kitchen smell amazing. Grilling the bread gives it a tasty char, but if you don't feel like turning on the grill you can also toast the bread.

Preheat the oven to 375°F.

Brush the flesh of the eggplant with a little of the olive oil and season with salt and pepper. Place the eggplant cut-sides down on a baking sheet and roast until the flesh begins to collapse, about 25 minutes. Remove and allow to rest until cool enough to handle. Scoop the flesh away from the skin and into a bowl and set aside.

Place the za'atar in a large, dry nonstick sauté pan over medium heat and toast until fragrant, about 30 seconds. Add the eggplant flesh and garlic confit to the pan and stir until warmed through. Season with salt and pepper and transfer to the bowl of a food processor fitted with the metal blade. Add the vinegar and lemon zest and puree until smooth.

Preheat a grill to high heat.

Brush the sliced bread on both sides with most of the rest of the olive oil (leaving 1 to 2 teaspoons) and place on the hot grill. Use tongs to turn the bread so that it grills evenly.

To serve, spread the eggplant puree on the grilled bread and top with the tomatoes. Season with salt and pepper, then top with the oregano and drizzle with the remaining olive oil. Cut each piece of bread into 3 or 4 bites.

1 small eggplant, stemmed and halved lengthwise

¼ cup extra-virgin olive oil

Kosher salt and freshly ground black pepper

½ teaspoon za'atar

1 tablespoon plus 1 teaspoon Garlic Confit (page 224)

3 tablespoons balsamic vinegar

½ teaspoon grated lemon zest

4 slices sourdough bread

1 pint medley cherry tomatoes, halved and sliced

1 teaspoon fresh oregano leaves

Chapter 5
Dinner

You know you've done a great job preparing a meal when you hear nothing but silence as the people you're cooking for sit and enjoy the food. I take as much pleasure knowing that people are enjoying the meal as much as I do making it. I love the whole process, starting with shopping for the ingredients all the way to presenting the meal. Cooking and sharing the food are equally important. Time passed with family and friends is always time well spent.

Dinner offers a natural occasion for getting together, and it tends to be a more elaborate meal than lunch. Planning dinner can be complex, especially if you are making multiple dishes. Any of the recipes in this chapter can serve as the focus. Start with the main and build the other components around it. The Rosemary Roasted Chicken with Pan Sauce (page 116) can go with several sides, like the Brussels Sprouts with Bacon and Parmesan (page 170) or the Scallion Mashed Potatoes (page 171). Feel free to mix and match. From there, write a checklist and plan ahead. A strong shopping list helps you organize. And be sure to have containers for any leftovers to make cleaning up easier.

I preach that recipes are guidelines rather than hard sets of rules—don't let little things become obstacles. Switch out the herbs or seasoning if you don't like them or don't have them. Change the cooking time depending on how it's going. Change the vegetables or garnish to suit your preferences. All recipes start somewhere and, over time, as you tweak them and make small changes to them, they become your own. That's how cooking becomes generational.

Scallops with Sautéed Corn and Miso Vinaigrette SERVES 4

WHEN SHOPPING FOR SCALLOPS, head to a reliable fishmonger and buy the scallops the day you plan to cook them. To prep, pull off the small adductor muscle that's attached to the meat of each scallop. Once you try this simple corn mixture, you'll want to pair it with all different types of seafood—and even eat it on its own.

Use a paring knife to shave the corn kernels from the cobs. Place a large sauté pan over high heat and add 2 tablespoons of the canola oil. Add the corn and sear until lightly colored, 2 to 3 minutes. Reduce the heat to medium-high and add the shallot, bell pepper, and garlic. Cook until the vegetables are softened, 4 to 5 minutes. Remove the pan from the heat and stir in the parsley butter and lemon zest. Season with salt and pepper and keep warm over low heat.

Pat the scallops dry and season with salt and pepper. Heat the remaining 2 tablespoons canola oil in another large sauté pan over medium-high heat. Sear the scallops until they just begin to brown on the bottom. Add the butter and push the scallops around the pan gently so they brown evenly. Reduce the heat to medium and turn the scallops. Cook for an additional 30 seconds, then remove the pan from the heat. Pour the lemon juice over the scallops and use a spoon to baste the scallops with the juices from the pan. Transfer the scallops from the pan to a paper towel–lined plate to blot any excess liquid.

Serve the scallops with the sautéed corn and drizzle with the miso vinaigrette.

3 ears corn, husks and silks removed

¼ cup canola oil

1 shallot, diced

1 red bell pepper, seeds and stem removed, diced

1 clove garlic, minced

2 tablespoons Parsley Butter (page 164)

Finely grated zest and juice of 1 lemon

Kosher salt and freshly ground black pepper

1 pound sea scallops

2 tablespoons unsalted butter

¾ cup Miso Vinaigrette (recipe follows)

Chef's Tip: Miso is fermented soybean paste frequently used in Japanese cooking. It is widely available in U.S. grocery stores. Use it to amp up flavor and add umami to your dishes.

Miso Vinaigrette MAKES ABOUT ¾ CUP

In a small mixing bowl, combine the garlic confit, ginger, lime juice, and soy sauce. With a fork, mash into a paste. Whisk in the remaining ingredients. Refrigerate until ready to use.

1 tablespoon Garlic Confit (page 224)

1 tablespoon grated fresh ginger

2 tablespoons freshly squeezed lime juice

2 tablespoons soy sauce

3 tablespoons white miso paste

1 tablespoon rice wine vinegar

1 tablespoon toasted sesame oil

1 tablespoon honey

1 teaspoon toasted sesame seeds (optional)

Grilled Tuna with Ginger Mustard and Tomato-Basil Salad **SERVES 4**

MUSTARD

¼ cup Dijon mustard

3 tablespoons crème fraîche

2 thumb-size pieces ginger, rinsed but unpeeled

½ teaspoon kosher salt

SALAD

1 medium red tomato

1 medium yellow tomato

Kosher salt and freshly ground black pepper

6 large basil leaves

2 tablespoons extra-virgin olive oil

TUNA

Four 6- to 7-ounce tuna steaks

2 tablespoons canola oil

Kosher salt and freshly ground black pepper

Juice of ½ lemon

12 small basil leaves

IN THE NORTHEAST, we get fresh local tuna from the summer into the fall. Tuna is one of the most consumed types of fish in the world and for good reason: it's versatile and delicious. Most fish counters feature a few species: bluefin, yellowfin, and bigeye. For this recipe, don't worry about the species—just look for nice, vibrant-looking steaks that are ready for the grill.

For the mustard, in a bowl combine the Dijon and crème fraîche. On the largest holes of a box grater, grate the ginger. Place a fine-mesh strainer over a small bowl. By hand, squeeze the ginger over the bowl to extract its juice. Discard solids and stir the ginger juice into the Dijon mixture. Stir in the salt. Cover and refrigerate until ready to serve.

For the salad, core the tomatoes. Slice the tomatoes into ½-inch-thick slices and then dice into ¼-inch pieces. Place the tomatoes and any juices in a mixing bowl and season with salt and pepper. Stack the basil leaves, roll into a tight cylinder, and slice into thin ribbons. Add to the tomatoes. Stir in the olive oil and let the salad sit at room temperature until ready to use.

For the tuna, preheat a grill to high heat and clean the grill grates.

Brush the tuna steaks with the canola oil and season liberally with salt and pepper. Place the tuna on the grill and cook for 90 seconds per side. Every 30 seconds, give the steaks a quarter turn to create even grill marks. The tuna should remain rare in the middle. (Adjust cooking time if you prefer your tuna cooked through.) Remove from the grill and drizzle the lemon juice over the tuna. Allow to rest for 5 minutes.

To show off the beautiful red interior of the tuna, slice each steak into 3 to 4 pieces. Place on individual plates, top with the tomato salad, and serve the ginger mustard on the side.

Rosemary Roasted Chicken with Pan Sauce

SERVES 4

A SIMPLE ROASTED CHICKEN is hard to beat. Culinary icons like Jacques Pépin have become legendary for their recipes for it, and if you've ever eaten Chef Pépin's chicken, you'll understand why. Rosemary adds a gentle floral flavor to the chicken both in the cavity and from the basting butter. Don't be put off by the high oven temperature. When roasting a chicken, I crank the heat up at first to get the skin crisp. It may create a little smoke, but that's just during the initial push. If you get to the end of the cooking time and the skin is not as crisp as you would like, raise the temperature again for the last 5 minutes or so. I recommend serving this with Scallion Mashed Potatoes (page 171) and Garlic and Lemon Green Beans (page 160). When you find a roast chicken recipe that you love, hang on to it. Hopefully this one will become yours.

6 sprigs rosemary

2 cloves garlic, crushed

One 2½- to 3-pound chicken, trussed

½ cup canola oil

Kosher salt and freshly ground black pepper

1 stick (8 tablespoons) unsalted butter

½ cup white wine

3 cups chicken stock

3 sprigs thyme

2 bay leaves

6 whole black peppercorns

Preheat the oven to 450°F.

Place 4 of the rosemary sprigs and the garlic cloves into the cavity of the chicken. Place the chicken on a rack set inside a roasting pan. Rub the canola oil all over the outside of the chicken and season liberally with salt and pepper. Roast in the oven for 15 minutes. Rotate the roasting pan and continue cooking 10 additional minutes.

While the chicken roasts, remove the leaves from the remaining 2 rosemary sprigs and chop finely. In a small saucepan, melt the butter over medium-low heat and add the chopped rosemary. Cook, stirring occasionally, until fragrant. It shouldn't take long.

Remove the chicken from the oven and brush half of the rosemary butter on the chicken. Reduce the oven temperature to 300°F and return the chicken to the oven. After 10 minutes, remove the chicken and brush with the remaining butter. Return the pan to the oven and continue roasting until the internal temperature of the meat reaches 165°F, about 15 additional minutes.

Remove the chicken from the oven, transfer to a cutting board, and let it rest for at least 20 minutes before carving.

Remove the rack from the roasting pan and discard the fat. Place the roasting pan on the stove over low heat and add the white wine. Whisk and scrape up any bits or drippings from the bottom of the pan. Raise

the heat to medium-high. When the liquid begins to boil, transfer it to a saucepan along with the chicken stock. Add the thyme sprigs, bay leaves, and peppercorns. Simmer for 20 minutes. Remove from the heat, strain (discard solids), and season with salt. Return to the saucepan and keep warm.

To carve the chicken, make a cut between a thigh and the breast and slice through to remove the leg. Repeat on the other side. Turn the chicken so that the point of the chicken breast is facing away from you and cut along the backbone of the chicken, keeping the skin intact. Slice along the backbone and ribs to remove each breast, and slice into 3 or 4 pieces. Remove the wings. Place all of the pieces on a serving platter and serve with the pan sauce on the side.

Chef's Tip: A few notes on roasting a chicken: Look for a smaller bird, not more than 3 pounds. Use a heavy-duty roasting pan equipped with a rack to allow the heat to circulate around the chicken. And don't dump the carcass—save the bones to make broth.

Chicken and Dumplings SERVES 4

THIS WAS A STAPLE in my house when I was growing up. It has humble roots—the very definition of homey—and is absolutely designed to be shared with friends and family. I had forgotten about this dish until one of my colleagues, Ally, made it for a staff meal one day. The aroma and taste brought me back to my childhood dinner table. You can chop the vegetables on the larger side, since they'll have lots of time to cook. And consider using an ice cream scoop to help portion the dumplings.

Preheat the oven to 325°F.

Heat the canola oil in a Dutch oven over medium-high heat. Season the chicken thighs with 1 teaspoon of the salt and a little pepper. Add them to the Dutch oven and sear until golden brown on both sides, 6 to 8 minutes. Transfer the thighs to a plate.

To the Dutch oven, add the carrot, onion, and celery. Sauté until they begin to soften, 4 to 5 minutes. Add the butter and garlic and cook, stirring frequently, until the butter is melted. With a wooden spoon or spatula, stir in ½ cup of the all-purpose flour about 1 tablespoon at a time, stirring and scraping the bottom of the pan so that nothing sticks between additions.

Add the stock 1 cup at a time, stirring with the spoon or spatula to combine between additions. Season with salt and pepper and break up any lumps. Add the thyme and rosemary. Cut the browned chicken thighs into 2 to 3 pieces each and add to the mixture. Bring to a simmer, cover with a lid, and transfer the pot to the oven. Cook for 30 minutes.

Meanwhile, make the dumplings. Place the milk in a medium bowl and whisk in the remaining 1½ cups all-purpose flour and the corn flour, the baking powder, and the remaining 1 teaspoon salt. Stir until the ingredients just come together; don't overmix.

Remove the pot from the oven and remove the lid. Use an ice cream scoop or large spoon to scoop ¼-cup portions of dumpling batter on top of the stew. The dumplings should cover the entire surface with just a little space between them. Raise the oven temperature to 400°F and place the pot, uncovered, back in the oven for 15 minutes. The dumplings should cook through and start to brown.

Remove from the oven and let sit for 5 to 10 minutes before serving.

3 tablespoons canola oil

2 pounds boneless, skinless chicken thighs

2 teaspoons kosher salt, plus more for seasoning

Freshly ground black pepper

1 medium carrot, diced

1 large Spanish onion, diced

2 ribs celery, diced

1 stick (8 tablespoons) unsalted butter

2 cloves garlic, minced

2 cups all-purpose flour

5 cups chicken stock

½ teaspoon chopped fresh thyme leaves

½ teaspoon chopped fresh rosemary leaves

1 cup whole milk

¼ cup corn flour

2 teaspoons baking powder

Chef's Tip: Corn flour is very finely ground cornmeal that adds texture. It's also gluten-free.

Crispy Duck Breast with Orange Sauce and Scallions SERVES 4

4 skin-on duck breasts

Kosher salt and freshly ground black pepper

3 tablespoons canola oil

4 scallions, white and green parts thinly sliced and kept separate

2 oranges, supremed and juices reserved

2 cups chicken stock

1 tablespoon unsalted butter

Chef's Tip: To supreme an orange—i.e., divide it into segments—remove the peel completely. Holding the orange over a fine-mesh strainer set in a bowl, cut with a paring knife between each segment, on either side of the white pith. The segments should come out easily. Let any juices fall through the strainer into the bowl. Once all the segments are loose, squeeze any remaining juice through the strainer as well.

COOKING DUCK IS EASIER than you think. While duck is poultry, it's cooked like red meat, meaning you don't have to cook it through as you would chicken or turkey. I like mine medium-rare. The key is to render the skin slowly to get it crisp and to allow the duck to rest for several minutes after cooking so that it retains its juices. Serve this with Caraway and Cumin Rice with Scallions (page 177).

Preheat the oven to 350°F.

Arrange the duck breasts on a cutting board, skin-sides down. Trim off any excess skin from around the meat of the breast; the skin should completely cover the meat but not hang off. Flip the breasts and score the skin with a sharp knife, but do not cut all the way down to the meat; make 3 to 4 vertical cuts and 3 to 4 horizontal cuts. Pat the breasts dry and season with salt and pepper.

In a large sauté pan, heat the canola oil over medium heat and place the duck skin-sides down in the pan. Cook slowly until the fat is rendered and the skin becomes crisp, 10 to 15 minutes. Transfer the duck skin-sides up to a rack placed over a baking sheet. Reserve the rendered duck fat in the pan. Roast the duck breasts in the oven for 5 minutes. Remove and let rest for about 10 minutes.

Meanwhile, pour out all but 1 tablespoon of the fat from the pan. Place the pan over medium heat. Add the scallion whites and sauté until they soften, 2 to 3 minutes. Add the juice from the orange segments and bring to a simmer. Add the chicken stock and simmer until the liquid is reduced by half. Reduce the heat to medium-low and whisk in the butter until melted. Stir in the orange segments and season with salt and pepper.

To slice the duck breasts, start at the thin end of one breast and cut through the skin at an angle to make ¼-inch slices. Repeat with each breast.

To serve, place the breasts on individual serving plates, pour the sauce over the breasts, and garnish with the scallion greens.

Chicken Cutlets with Garlicky Spinach **SERVES 4**

YOU CAN MAKE QUICK WORK of pan-fried breaded chicken if you take a minute to prep all of your ingredients in advance. I like to season my own breadcrumbs, but you can also purchase seasoned breadcrumbs as a shortcut. Remember that the spinach will wilt down to almost nothing, so you need to start with a lot.

For the chicken, pound the chicken breasts between two pieces of plastic wrap or parchment paper with a mallet so they are of even thickness. In the bowl of a food processor fitted with the metal blade, combine the panko, turmeric, oregano, garlic powder, onion powder, salt, and pepper and pulse to combine. Transfer to a wide shallow bowl.

Place the flour in another shallow bowl and in a third shallow bowl, beat the eggs. Dredge a piece of chicken in the flour and shake off any excess. Dredge it in the egg and let the excess run off. Place it in the breadcrumbs and press to coat. Set on a plate and repeat with the remaining chicken, flour, egg, and breadcrumbs. Refrigerate for 5 to 10 minutes.

Preheat the oven to 300°F.

Place the canola oil in a large sauté pan over medium-high heat. When the oil is hot, cook the chicken, working in batches, if necessary, to avoid crowding the pan, until golden brown, 3 to 5 minutes per side. Transfer the chicken to a baking sheet and keep warm in the oven while you make the sauce and spinach.

For the sauce, add the chicken stock to the sauté pan used to brown the cutlets. Bring to a boil over high heat and reduce to about 1 cup, scraping up the browned bits. Reduce the heat to medium-high and add the cream. Simmer until reduced to about 1½ cups. Whisk in the mustard and season with salt and pepper.

For the spinach, in a large sauté pan, place the garlic confit over medium heat and cook until fragrant, about 30 seconds. Add the spinach and cook, stirring, until just wilted but not mushy. Remove from the heat and stir in the lemon juice. Season with salt and pepper.

To serve, place the spinach on a large platter and place the chicken cutlets on top. Serve the sauce and lemon wedges on the side.

CHICKEN

Four 5-ounce boneless, skinless chicken breasts

2 cups panko breadcrumbs

1 teaspoon ground turmeric

1 teaspoon dried oregano

½ teaspoon garlic powder

½ teaspoon onion powder

1 teaspoon kosher salt

½ teaspoon freshly ground black pepper

1 cup all-purpose flour

2 large eggs

½ cup canola oil

6 lemon wedges

SAUCE

2 cups chicken stock

2 cups heavy cream

2 tablespoons grainy mustard

Kosher salt and freshly ground black pepper

SPINACH

2 tablespoons Garlic Confit (page 224)

2 pounds spinach

1 tablespoon freshly squeezed lemon juice

Kosher salt and freshly ground black pepper

Pork Loin Schnitzel with Arugula and Creamy Shiitake Mushroom Sauce SERVES 4

Four 5-ounce slices pork loin

Kosher salt and freshly ground black pepper

2 cups panko breadcrumbs

¼ teaspoon grated nutmeg

½ teaspoon dry mustard

1 cup all-purpose flour

2 large eggs, beaten with 2 tablespoons room-temperature water

½ cup canola oil

2 cups arugula

2 tablespoons freshly squeezed lemon juice

3 tablespoons extra-virgin olive oil

1¼ cups Creamy Shiitake Mushroom Sauce (recipe follows)

ONE OF THE TRADITIONAL WAYS to serve Austria's famed schnitzel is with "hunter," or mushroom, sauce. This is my variation on that classic. I pair the earthy flavors of mushrooms and pork with a sharp arugula salad. Use restraint when pounding the pork loins—they should be about ¼ inch thick. Don't be put off by the amount of oil used to cook the shiitakes—you want them crisp, and any excess fat is poured off. The sauce can be prepared one day in advance.

Preheat the oven to 250ºF.

Pound the pork slices between two pieces of plastic wrap or parchment paper with a mallet so they are an even ¼ inch thick. Season lightly with salt and pepper.

Place the panko, nutmeg, and dry mustard in the bowl of a food processor fitted with the metal blade and pulse until fine. Set up a breading station by placing the flour, the egg mixture, and the breadcrumb mixture into three separate shallow bowls.

Dredge one slice of pork in the flour and shake off any excess. Dip into the egg mixture and let the excess drip off. Place in the breadcrumbs and press to coat. Repeat with remaining pork, flour, egg, and breadcrumbs.

Heat the canola oil in a large sauté pan over medium-high heat. Working in batches, if necessary to avoid crowding the pan, add the breaded pork and brown until crispy, 2 to 3 minutes on the first side and 1 minute on the second side. Transfer the pork to a rack set on a baking sheet and place in the oven to keep warm.

In a medium bowl, toss the arugula with the lemon juice and olive oil. Season with salt and pepper.

Just before serving, remove the pork from the oven and season with salt and pepper. Place the cutlets on a platter and top with the arugula salad. Serve the sauce on the side.

Creamy Shiitake Mushroom Sauce

MAKES ABOUT 1¼ CUPS

1 cup canola oil

1 pound shiitake mushrooms, stemmed and thinly sliced

1 large shallot, minced

2 cloves garlic, minced

½ cup white wine

1 cup chicken stock

1 cup heavy cream

Kosher salt and freshly ground black pepper

2 tablespoons freshly squeezed lemon juice

In a large sauté pan, heat the canola oil over medium-high heat. Working in batches, if necessary to avoid crowding the pan, add the mushrooms and sauté, stirring frequently, until crisp, 4 to 5 minutes. Use a slotted spoon to transfer the mushrooms to a plate. Pour off all but 1 teaspoon of oil.

Return the pan to medium heat. Add the shallot and garlic to the pan and cook for 30 seconds. Add the white wine and simmer until it has nearly evaporated. Add the chicken stock and cream and simmer until the liquid reduces by half. Return the mushrooms to the pan and simmer for 6 minutes.

Remove the pan from the heat, season the sauce with salt and pepper, and stir in the lemon juice.

Roasted Rack of Lamb with Barley and Pearl Onions   SERVES 4

RACK OF LAMB IS a special meal suited to a celebration. It's an expensive cut of meat but, in my opinion, one of the tastiest. When ordering the rack, ask the butcher to keep a little of the fat cap in place. Also, be sure to use a meat thermometer to gauge doneness—I like lamb just past medium-rare.

For the barley, in a small stockpot, heat the canola oil over medium heat and add the onion. Sauté until it begins to color, 3 to 4 minutes. Add the barley and stir to coat. Stir in the apple and thyme and the 5 cups chicken stock and bring to a simmer. Add the bay leaves and 1 tablespoon sea salt and a few grinds of black pepper. Simmer until the barley is tender and looks creamy, about 20 minutes. If the barley is not yet cooked and it begins to look dry, add more chicken stock as needed. Taste and adjust salt. Keep warm.

For the onions, prepare an ice bath as on page 225. Fill a medium saucepan with water, season with salt, and bring to a boil. Add the onions and cook for 1 minute. Transfer the onions to the ice bath. Once cool, drain and squeeze each onion to remove the skin.

In a large sauté pan over medium-high heat, cook the bacon until crisp. Use a slotted spoon to transfer to a paper towel–lined plate, leaving the rendered bacon fat in the pan. Add the butter and sugar to the pan and cook, stirring frequently, until beginning to turn a caramel color. Add the onions and stir to coat well. Add the vinegar and bring to a boil. Add the chicken stock and reduce the heat to medium. Simmer until the onions are soft and glazed, 8 to 10 minutes. Return the bacon to the pan, stir to combine, and season with salt and pepper. Keep warm.

(continues on page 131)

BARLEY

3 tablespoons canola oil

1 small Spanish onion, cut into small dice

2 cups pearled barley

1 honeycrisp apple, cored, peeled, and diced

1 teaspoon chopped thyme

5 cups chicken stock, plus more as needed

2 bay leaves

1 tablespoon sea salt, plus more as needed

Freshly ground black pepper

ONIONS

Kosher salt

2 cups pearl onions, trimmed

3 thick-cut strips bacon, cut into small dice

2 tablespoons unsalted butter

3 tablespoons granulated sugar

¼ cup balsamic vinegar

½ cup chicken stock

Freshly ground black pepper

LAMB

¼ cup canola oil

2 trimmed racks of lamb, 8 bones each

Kosher salt and freshly ground black pepper

1 tablespoon Dijon mustard

1 teaspoon chopped fresh rosemary leaves

1 teaspoon chopped garlic

Sea salt

For the lamb, preheat the oven to 325°F.

In a sauté pan that's large enough for one rack of lamb to lie flat, heat the canola oil over medium-high heat. Add one rack to the pan, fat-side down, and sear until the fat renders and the rack turns golden brown, 3 to 4 minutes. Flip the rack and sear for 1 minute on the loin side. Transfer to a rack set on a baking sheet. Repeat with the remaining rack of lamb. Blot the meat with a paper towel to remove any surface fat. Season with kosher salt and pepper.

In a small bowl, combine the Dijon, rosemary, and garlic. Rub the mixture all over the lamb. Transfer the baking sheet to the oven and roast for 12 minutes. Rotate the baking sheet and cook until it has reached the temperature you prefer. (For medium-rare, roast until the thermometer reads 130°F to 135°F, about 6 additional minutes.) Remove from the oven and allow to sit for 15 minutes before carving.

To serve, place the barley in a serving dish and spoon the pearl onions and any liquid in the pan over the top. Slice the lamb racks between each bone to create individual chops and place them on a serving platter. Season each chop with sea salt just before serving.

Slow-Roasted Pork Shoulder with Black Beans
SERVES 4 TO 6

PORK

One 5-pound boneless pork shoulder with fat cap

½ cup freshly squeezed orange juice

1 small Spanish onion, chopped

4 cloves garlic

¼ cup extra-virgin olive oil

2 tablespoons chopped fresh rosemary leaves

2 teaspoons smoked paprika

Kosher salt and freshly ground black pepper

Juice of 1 lime

1 lime cut into wedges

BEANS

2 cups dried black beans, soaked for 2 hours

Kosher salt

3 tablespoons canola oil

1 Spanish onion, cut into small dice

1 red bell pepper, seeded and cut into small dice

3 cloves garlic, minced

1 jalapeño pepper, seeded and minced

6 cups vegetable stock or room temperature water

Freshly ground black pepper

I FIND JOY IN the simplicity of slow-roasted meats. This dish takes several hours, but you don't need to hover over it, so you can do other things around the house while it's cooking. You can, of course, use canned beans if you're in a hurry, but I highly recommend cooking your own beans, as they're more flavorful. Be sure to purchase a pork shoulder with the fat cap still on. Leftovers of this dish are excellent and marry well with the Roasted Broccoli Rabe and Calabrian Chile and Lemon (page 156).

For the pork, trim the pork shoulder's fat cap so that there is an even layer of fat over the meat and place the shoulder in a large stainless steel or glass bowl. In a blender, combine the orange juice, onion, garlic, olive oil, rosemary, and paprika and puree until smooth. Pour the mixture over the pork and rub it into the meat. Cover loosely with plastic wrap and refrigerate for 4 to 8 hours.

Preheat the oven to 425ºF.

Remove the pork from the marinade and let the excess run off, but don't scrape off the marinade. Set the pork fat-side up in a large, lidded baking dish or Dutch oven. Season the meat on all sides with salt and pepper. Roast in the oven, uncovered, for 20 minutes. Reduce the temperature to 300ºF and cover the pan with the lid. Cook for 4 more hours.

Meanwhile, make the beans. Rinse the beans under cold water and place them in a medium saucepan with cold water to cover. Season with salt. Place over high heat and bring to a boil. Immediately remove the pan from the heat and drain. Clean out the saucepan and set aside. In a large sauté pan, heat the canola oil over medium heat and add the onion and bell pepper. Sauté for 1 minute. Add the garlic and jalapeño and cook for another 30 seconds. Place the drained black beans back in the clean saucepan and add the cooked vegetables and the stock and bring to a boil. Reduce the heat until the mixture is simmering gently and cook until the beans are tender, 50 to 60 minutes. Remove from the heat. Transfer 2 cups of cooking liquid and beans to a blender and puree until smooth. Fold the puree back into the beans. Season with salt and pepper.

(continues on page 134)

Remove the pork from the oven and let sit until the meat is cool enough to handle. Remove the fat cap completely and use forks or your hands to pull the pork apart into shreds. Season the meat with a little salt and the lime juice.

To serve, place a large spoonful of beans on each individual plate and top with shredded pork. Garnish with lime wedges.

Pasta with Asparagus, Pecorino, and Black Pepper SERVES 4

MAKE THIS SIMPLE YET satisfying dish in the spring when asparagus is in season. Trim an inch or two off the thick, tough end of each stalk. Aleppo pepper lends a little heat. Use a light hand when seasoning as some pecorino can be salty.

Bring a pot of salted water to a boil and add the pasta. Cook until just al dente (usually 1 to 2 minutes less than the package instructions). Reserve ½ cup of the cooking liquid and drain the pasta.

Meanwhile, trim the bottom 1 to 2 inches off of the asparagus stalks. Slice the asparagus at an angle ¼ inch thick, leaving the tips intact.

In a large sauté pan, heat the olive oil over medium heat. Sauté the asparagus slices (reserving the tips) until they begin to color around the edges, 2 to 3 minutes. Add the shallot and garlic. Cook until they're softened, 2 to 3 minutes. Add the reserved pasta cooking liquid and bring to a boil. Whisk in half the pecorino along with the butter and black pepper and season with salt. Add the cooked pasta and asparagus tips and stir until heated through.

Remove the pan from the heat and add the lemon juice. Transfer the pasta to a serving dish and top with the remaining pecorino, the parsley, and the Aleppo pepper.

Kosher salt

1 pound dried casarecce

1 bunch asparagus

3 tablespoons extra-virgin olive oil

1 small shallot, minced

1 tablespoon minced garlic

½ cup finely grated pecorino

2 tablespoons unsalted butter

1 teaspoon freshly ground black pepper

1 tablespoon freshly squeezed lemon juice

2 tablespoons chopped flat-leaf parsley

½ teaspoon Aleppo pepper

Super Ramen SERVES 4 TO 6

BROTH

6 scallions

4 ounces whole shiitake
   mushrooms

8 cups chicken or vegetable
   stock

2 cloves garlic, smashed

1 thumb-size piece ginger,
   thinly sliced

3 tablespoons white miso

TOPPINGS

2 pounds boneless, skinless
   chicken breasts

Kosher salt and freshly ground
   black pepper

3 tablespoons canola oil

Reserved shiitake caps

2 medium carrots, sliced

1 red bell pepper, seeded and
   thinly sliced

1 small red onion, thinly sliced

1 rib celery, sliced

2 heads baby bok choy

1 tablespoon grated fresh ginger

1 tablespoon chopped garlic

2 cups baby spinach

3 tablespoons soy sauce

2 tablespoons rice wine vinegar

NOODLES AND FINISHING

Kosher salt

4 ounces dried ramen noodles

1 tablespoon toasted sesame oil

Reserved scallion greens, thinly
   sliced

1 tablespoon toasted sesame
   seeds

4 to 6 Sunny-Side Up eggs
   (page 228), 2 tablespoons
   sambal sauce, and/or 1 tablespoon togarashi (optional)

MY WHOLE FAMILY LOVES RAMEN. This recipe is far from traditional ramen, but I started making it when my kids were very young as a way to get them to eat more vegetables and learn how to use chopsticks. Originally, I just used packets of Top Ramen brand ramen and supplemented it with lots of vegetables, but over the years the dish has evolved into what I like to call super ramen, and it's now the most requested meal I make at home. If you have young kids, you might want to take it easy on the miso or leave it out altogether; as their palates evolve, you can add more elements. The idea is to make it fun and approachable. If you have a wok, now is the time to use it.

To make the broth, cut the green parts off each scallion (reserve for finishing) and thinly slice the white parts. Place the white parts in a large stockpot. Remove the caps from the shiitakes and reserve for the toppings. Add the stems to the pot. Add the stock, garlic, and ginger to the pot and place over medium-high heat. Simmer for 15 minutes. Remove the pot from the heat and let cool for 1 hour. Whisk in the miso paste, then strain the liquid through a fine-mesh strainer into a large bowl. Cover and refrigerate until ready to use or keep warm while you prep everything else.

To make the toppings, preheat the oven to 300°F.

Season the chicken breasts with salt and pepper and place on a baking sheet. Cover the sheet with foil and bake until the chicken is completely cooked, about 40 minutes. Remove from the oven and let cool. Dice the chicken into small pieces and set aside.

Heat the canola oil in a large wok or sauté pan over medium-high heat. Slice the reserved shiitake caps and add to the wok. Cook until they begin to crisp around the edges. Add the carrots, bell pepper, onion, and celery. Raise the heat to high and cook until the vegetables soften, 3 to 4 minutes. Add the bok choy, ginger, and garlic and cook until the bok choy is tender, 3 to 4 minutes. Add the broth in a thin stream, then simmer for 10 minutes. Remove the wok from the heat. Stir in the cooked chicken breast, spinach, soy sauce, and rice wine vinegar.

To make the noodles, bring a pot of salted water to a boil and add the noodles. Cook until tender, 3 to 4 minutes. Drain the noodles, then divide them among the serving bowls and ladle the vegetables and broth over the top. Finish each bowl with a drizzle of sesame oil, scallion greens, and sesame seeds. If desired, top each with an egg, a dab of sambal, and/or a sprinkle of togarashi.

Cauliflower and Bacon Pasta SERVES 4

BACON AND CAULIFLOWER are a stellar combination. Add cheese and pasta and it's a party. This straightforward dish can be prepped in advance, making it a breeze to put together. I call for cavatelli here but just about any dried pasta will work.

Heat the canola oil in a large sauté pan over medium heat. Add the bacon and cook until crisp. Use a slotted spoon to transfer the bacon to a paper towel–lined plate, leaving the rendered fat in the pan. Add the cauliflower and sauté until it begins to color and soften, 3 to 4 minutes. Use a spoon to hold back the contents of the pan and pour out and discard most of the fat. Return the pan to the heat and add the shallots and garlic. Cook until the shallots are softened, about 2 minutes. Add the chicken stock, raise the heat to medium-high, and simmer for 5 minutes.

Bring a pot of salted water to a boil and cook the pasta according to package instructions. Drain, then add the pasta to the pan with the cauliflower. Add the cooked bacon and sherry vinegar and season with salt and pepper. Cook, stirring occasionally, until the mixture is hot and fully combined. Transfer to a serving bowl and top with the Parmesan, parsley, and chili flakes.

2 tablespoons canola oil

½ pound thick-cut bacon, diced

1 small head cauliflower, cut into small florets

2 shallots, minced

2 cloves garlic, chopped

1 cup chicken stock

Kosher salt

1 pound dried cavatelli

1 tablespoon sherry vinegar

Freshly ground black pepper

¼ cup grated Parmesan

2 tablespoons chopped flat-leaf parsley leaves

1 teaspoon chili flakes

Spaghetti with Littleneck Clams and Black Pepper Butter SERVES 4

Kosher salt

1 pound spaghetti

24 littleneck clams

2 tablespoons canola oil

1 Spanish onion, cut into small
    dice

2 tablespoons Garlic Confit
    (page 224)

½ cup white wine

3 tablespoons roughly chopped
    flat-leaf parsley leaves

3 tablespoons Black Pepper
    Butter (page 196)

2 tablespoons freshly squeezed
    lemon juice

¼ cup grated Parmesan

CLAMS ARE FORGIVING and they cook quickly. The only thing that can ruin this dish is sand in the clams. Make sure you hand scrub each clam and rinse them well under cold running water, but don't just soak them in water as that will cause them to die. Buy the clams the day you plan to use them. Timing this dish is the trickiest part—you want all the items to be cooked at about the same time.

Bring a large pot of salted water to a boil. Add the spaghetti and cook until just al dente, 6 to 7 minutes. (It will finish cooking in the sauce.) Drain and set aside.

In a medium saucepan with a tight-fitting lid, combine the clams with 1 cup water. Cover and place over medium heat. Simmer until all the clams open, about 5 minutes. (Remove and discard any unopened clams.) Remove from the heat and set aside, reserving the clams and their cooking liquid.

In a large sauté pan, heat the canola oil over medium heat and sauté the onion until it begins to color. Stir in the garlic confit and then the white wine. Simmer until the wine has nearly completely evaporated. Remove 1 cup of the clam cooking liquid. If there is any sand left from cooking the clams, it will have settled at the bottom, so pour the liquid off slowly, while holding back the clams with a spoon and leave a little liquid with the clams. Add the 1 cup clam cooking liquid to the sauté pan.

Simmer the onion mixture for 1 minute. Add the cooked pasta, parsley, and black pepper butter to the pan. Stir to combine and simmer for 30 seconds. Season with salt and add the lemon juice.

To serve, place the pasta in a large serving bowl. Place the clams on top. Sprinkle on the Parmesan.

Pasta with Meatballs and Red Sauce **SERVES 4**

MAKING GREAT MEATBALLS isn't difficult. I don't mind chicken and turkey versions, but honestly, the fat in pork and beef gives meatballs both flavor and texture. I put the meatballs in the fridge after they've been formed to firm them up before cooking. You'll know you've put good meatballs onto the table when everyone quiets down and digs in.

In a large sauté pan, heat the olive oil over medium heat and add the onion. Sauté until the onion begins to color, 2 to 3 minutes. Stir in the garlic and cook until fragrant, about 30 seconds. Remove the pan from the heat and stir in the sage and rosemary. Let the mixture rest until it reaches room temperature.

In the bowl of a stand mixer fitted with the paddle attachment, combine the beef, pork, egg, breadcrumbs, sour cream, ricotta, and ¼ cup of the Parmesan. Mix on medium speed until combined. Add the sautéed onion mixture, the 1 tablespoon salt, and the pepper. Mix for another 30 seconds.

Take 1 ounce of the meat mixture in your hands, roll it into a sphere, and place it on a baking sheet. Repeat with the remaining mixture. Refrigerate for 1 hour.

Preheat the oven to 450°F.

Transfer the baking sheet to the oven and bake for 8 minutes. Reduce the temperature to 300°F and continue baking for 5 additional minutes. Remove the meatballs from the oven and let them sit at room temperature.

Meanwhile, place the tomato sauce in a large saucepan over medium-low heat and cook until it just begins to bubble. Reduce the heat and keep warm. Bring a large pot of salted water to a boil and cook the pasta to al dente, 1 to 2 minutes less than what the package instructs. Drain the pasta and return it to the pot. Add half of the warmed tomato sauce to the pasta and stir to combine. Place the meatballs in the saucepan with the remaining tomato sauce and stir to combine. Raise the heat to medium and cook, stirring frequently, until the meatballs are completely warmed through.

To serve, transfer the pasta to a large serving bowl and carefully spoon the meatballs and remaining sauce over top. Tear the basil leaves and scatter on top of the pasta. Sprinkle on the remaining ¼ cup Parmesan and the chili flakes.

2 tablespoons extra-virgin olive oil

1 small Spanish onion, minced

2 cloves garlic, chopped

2 teaspoons chopped fresh sage leaves

1 teaspoon chopped fresh rosemary leaves

8 ounces ground beef

8 ounces ground pork

1 large egg

½ cup breadcrumbs

3 tablespoons sour cream

3 tablespoons ricotta

½ cup finely grated Parmesan

1 tablespoon kosher salt, plus more for pasta water

1 teaspoon freshly ground black pepper

4 cups Tomato Sauce (page 226)

1 pound rigatoni

12 basil leaves

½ teaspoon chili flakes

Chef's Tip: My secret ingredients in meatballs are sour cream and ricotta. They lend a unique flavor and a creamier texture.

Chapter 6
Vegetables and Sides

Vegetables offer a creative outlet for chefs and have become a focus on many restaurant menus. As that shift has trickled down to home kitchens, they've taken center stage on the dinner table. The little gems in this chapter are meant to complement or be a part of the meal—or they can also be put together to make a meal on their own.

Cooking vegetables and starches correctly can be just as challenging as cooking protein—and just as rewarding. Start simply and make sure you season. There's nothing worse than bland vegetables, like the ones I ate as a kid.

We have so much access to a great variety of vegetables and grains these days. (When did Brussels sprouts become so popular? They were like a punishment for me as a kid, and now they're seemingly beloved by everyone.) To make vegetable cookery even more fun, head to a farmer's market and buy directly from the person growing the ingredients. I guarantee it will improve your enjoyment of the dish.

Grilled Asparagus with Orange and Watercress

SERVES 4 AS A SIDE

2 bunches asparagus

3 tablespoons extra-virgin olive oil

Kosher salt and freshly ground black pepper

1 cup watercress

2 oranges, supremed (see Chef's Tip on page 122) and juices reserved

¼ cup Pickled Shallots (see Chef's Tip on page 99)

Chef's Tip: Peel the tough skin off the bottom few inches of each stalk of thicker asparagus with a vegetable peeler or a paring knife.

WHEN ASPARAGUS STARTS to turn up at the farmer's market in the spring, it's a sign that winter has truly ended. I know imported asparagus is available in the grocery store year-round, but for this dish, where the spears are the star, you need fresh asparagus purchased in season. Look for larger stalks that will stand up to grilling, but if they are jumbo-size, peel the stalks before cooking. (See the tip below.) Watercress has a peppery bite, but you could also use arugula or mizuna in its place.

Heat a grill to medium-high.

Place the asparagus spears on a cutting board so all the tips are lined up. Cut the bottom 1 to 2 inches from each asparagus spear and discard. Transfer the trimmed spears to a baking sheet or tray and drizzle 2 tablespoons of the olive oil over the asparagus. Roll the pieces around to coat. Season with salt and pepper.

Place the asparagus on the hot grill, positioning the spears perpendicular to the grates so that they don't fall through or get stuck. Use tongs to turn the asparagus frequently. Once the asparagus are slightly charred and tender but still firm, remove from the grill and place on a serving platter.

In a medium bowl, toss together the watercress, orange segments and juice, pickled shallots, and remaining 1 tablespoon olive oil. Season with salt and pepper to taste. Place the salad on top of the asparagus and serve.

Curry-Roasted Cauliflower with Chickpeas

SERVES 4 AS A SIDE

THIS IS A FULL-FLAVORED vegetarian dish that you can set in the center of the table for sharing—just be sure to provide each diner with a knife, a spoon, and crusty bread to soak up the juices. There are a lot of big flavors here, especially in the vinaigrette. Black garlic is easy to find these days—it has a sweet, pungent flavor that complements vegetables and seafood. Note that the vinaigrette may look broken but that's okay—just give it a good stir right before serving.

Preheat the oven to 350°F.

In a small bowl, stir together the olive oil and curry powder. Brush half of the mixture on all sides of the cauliflower. Season with salt and pepper. Place the cauliflower crown-side down in a cast-iron pan or baking dish. Roast in the oven for 12 minutes. Remove from the oven and turn crown-side up. Drizzle the remaining curry oil over the top.

Place the red onion, tomato, and chickpeas around the cauliflower and bake for 10 additional minutes. Add the vegetable stock and continue baking for an additional 25 minutes. Remove from the oven and season with salt and pepper.

To serve, drizzle some of the vinaigrette over the top and garnish with the lemon zest and parsley. Serve in the pan or baking dish and pass the remaining vinaigrette on the side.

¼ cup extra-virgin olive oil

2 teaspoons curry powder

1 small head cauliflower, trimmed and core removed

Kosher salt and freshly ground black pepper

1 small red onion, thinly sliced (about ½ cup)

1 beefsteak tomato, cored and diced

1 cup Cooked Chickpeas (page 230)

½ cup vegetable stock

½ cup Black Garlic Vinaigrette (recipe follows)

1 teaspoon grated lemon zest

1 tablespoon chopped flat-leaf parsley leaves

Black Garlic Vinaigrette

MAKES ABOUT ½ CUP

In a bowl, mash the garlic and Dijon into a paste. Whisk in the vinegar and then add the oil in a thin stream while whisking. Season with salt and pepper. Refrigerate until ready to use.

6 cloves black garlic, peeled

1 teaspoon Dijon mustard

2 tablespoons champagne vinegar

¼ cup plus 2 tablespoons extra-virgin olive oil

Kosher salt and freshly ground black pepper

Chef's Tip: Black garlic is aged for several weeks in controlled conditions. It takes on a fermented odor and a unique, slightly sour flavor. Find it in specialty markets or online.

Sautéed Greens with Smoked Almonds and Apples

SERVES 4 AS A SIDE

1 bunch red Swiss chard, stems removed and reserved and leaves chopped

2 tablespoons extra-virgin olive oil

1 large shallot, thinly sliced

1 bunch kale, stemmed and chopped

1 honeycrisp apple

½ teaspoon chili flakes

1 tablespoon freshly squeezed lemon juice

Kosher salt and freshly ground black pepper

½ cup smoked almonds, coarsely crushed

BESIDES BEING TASTY, greens are good for you. Always wash and dry your greens before cooking—rushing the process may end with grit in your dish. Peel and dice the apple at the last minute so it doesn't turn brown.

Trim off the bottom few inches of the Swiss chard stems. Thinly slice the remaining stems. In a large sauté pan, heat the olive oil over medium heat and add the sliced stems and shallot. Sauté until they begin to soften. Add the kale and chopped chard and sauté until the leaves are soft and tender, 2 to 3 minutes.

Meanwhile, peel, core, and dice the apple. Stir the apple and chili flakes into the pan. Remove from the heat. Drizzle on the lemon juice and season with salt and pepper. Transfer to a serving dish and sprinkle the smoked almonds over the top. Serve hot.

Turmeric-Roasted Carrots with Whipped Feta and Toasted Pistachios SERVES 4 AS A SIDE

FOR A BEAUTIFUL PRESENTATION, I like to use multicolored carrots with the tops still on. (You can also use carrots without the tops; it'll still taste great.) I like the tang of feta against the pistachios, but you can substitute goat cheese or use any other nut here as well. If you whip the feta in advance, be sure to let it sit at room temperature for about one hour before serving.

Preheat the oven to 350°F.

In the bowl of a food processor fitted with the metal blade, combine the feta and cream cheese and puree until smooth. Add the cream and puree for another 30 seconds. Use a flexible rubber spatula to transfer the mixture to a bowl. Set aside at room temperature.

Trim the tops of the carrots down to 3 to 4 inches and rinse to remove any dirt. Pat dry and arrange in a single layer on a rimmed baking sheet. In a small bowl, combine the garlic confit and turmeric and use a brush to coat the carrots with the mixture. Season with salt and pepper. Roast the carrots until cooked through but still with a little crunch, about 12 minutes. Transfer the carrots to a plate and reserve any oil left on the baking sheet.

Place the pistachios on the baking sheet and return to the oven for 6 minutes. Allow to cool slightly, then chop with a knife.

To serve, spread the whipped feta on a platter and place the carrots on top. Drizzle the oil from the baking sheet over the carrots and garnish with the pistachios.

½ cup feta

¼ cup cream cheese

¼ cup heavy cream

12 to 16 medium carrots with tops intact

¼ cup Garlic Confit (page 224)

1 tablespoon ground turmeric

Kosher salt and freshly ground black pepper

¾ cup pistachios

Baked Tomatoes with Zucchini and Ricotta

SERVES 4 AS A SIDE OR AS A LIGHT MAIN

4 large ripe tomatoes, each about the size of a tennis ball

2 small zucchini

2 tablespoons canola oil

2 large cloves garlic, chopped

Kosher salt and freshly ground black pepper

1 cup ricotta

2 tablespoons chopped fresh oregano leaves

Grated zest of 1 lemon

2 tablespoons grated Parmesan

1 tablespoon extra-virgin olive oil

THIS IS A GREAT WAY to use two summer vegetables at their peak. Select tomatoes of uniform size so they cook evenly. You can omit the ricotta and top these with just the grated Parmesan. The whole dish can be prepared a day ahead and baked just before serving.

Use a sharp knife to slice a thin piece off the bottom of each tomato so they sit flat. Remove a thin slice from the top of the tomato and scoop out the seeds, juice, and any pieces of flesh that come out easily while keeping the tomatoes intact. Transfer the pulp and juices to a bowl and mash with a fork.

Trim and halve the zucchini crosswise. Stand the halves up vertically and slice down on each side, taking off the skin along with about ½ inch of flesh, so you're cutting out the seedy core from the inside. Repeat three times so you have 4 flat slices of zucchini from each half. Dice the zucchini into ¼-inch pieces.

Heat the canola oil in a sauté pan over medium heat and add the diced zucchini. Cook until it begins to brown, 4 to 5 minutes. Add the garlic and cook until fragrant, about 30 seconds. Remove the pan from the heat and drain off any excess oil. Add the tomato pulp to the pan and return to medium heat. Simmer until most of the liquid has evaporated. Remove from the heat and season with salt and pepper.

Preheat the oven to 375°F.

In a mixing bowl, combine the ricotta with the oregano and lemon zest. Season with salt and pepper. Spoon the cooked zucchini into each tomato and top with the ricotta mixture. Evenly sprinkle the Parmesan over the tomatoes, drizzle them with the olive oil, and place them in a high-sided casserole dish. Bake for 15 minutes. Serve hot.

Roasted Broccoli Rabe with Calabrian Chili and Lemon

SERVES 4 AS A SIDE

2 bunches broccoli rabe, trimmed

2 tablespoons extra-virgin olive oil

Kosher salt and freshly ground black pepper

Grated zest and juice of 1 lemon

2 tablespoons crushed Calabrian chili

Chef's Tip: You'll find plenty of other uses for Calabrian chili, such as on top of eggs, as a substitute for salsa verde or pesto, and mixed with sour cream for a terrific dip.

THE SWEET HEAT of Calabrian chili (sold in jars and packed in oil) balances the bite of broccoli rabe.

Preheat the oven to 375°F.

Spread the broccoli rabe in a single layer on a baking sheet. Toss with the olive oil and season with salt and pepper. Bake for 12 minutes. Remove from the oven and drizzle with the lemon juice. Toss the broccoli rabe to combine it with the oil on the baking sheet. Transfer to a serving dish, and scatter the chili and lemon zest over the top.

Snap Peas in Ginger and Garlic SERVES 4 AS A SIDE

FRESH SNAP PEAS ARE delicious. I like to eat them raw, but they're also great cooked. You can blanch the peas in advance and keep them refrigerated until you're ready to make the dish, but do it the same day you plan to serve them so they stay bright and fresh-looking. Peas that are really large tend to be tough, so seek out small- to medium-size pea pods.

Prepare an ice bath as on page 225. Blanch the peas in salted boiling water for 1 to 2 minutes. (See page 225 for instructions. Leave them slightly undercooked.) Transfer to the ice bath, then drain and set aside.

Combine the olive oil and ginger in a large sauté pan over medium heat and cook, stirring, until the ginger is fragrant, about 30 seconds. Add the garlic confit and cook until fragrant. Add the peas and stir to combine until the peas are coated and heated through, 3 to 4 minutes. Remove from the heat, stir in the lemon zest, and season with salt and pepper. Serve hot.

4 cups sugar snap peas, strings removed (see Chef's Tip on page 79)

Kosher salt

2 tablespoons extra-virgin olive oil

2 teaspoons grated ginger

1 tablespoon Garlic Confit (page 224)

1 teaspoon grated lemon zest

Freshly ground black pepper

Garlic and Lemon Green Beans SERVES 4 AS A SIDE

1 pound string beans, trimmed

Kosher salt

2 tablespoons extra-virgin
    olive oil

2 cloves garlic, minced

¼ cup vegetable stock or room
    temperature water

1 teaspoon grated lemon zest

1 tablespoon freshly squeezed
    lemon juice

Freshly ground black pepper

DON'T SLEEP ON GREEN BEANS—they are one of the true gems of summer. I use traditional string beans in this recipe, but yellow wax, purple, and Romano beans are also great. Be careful not to overcook them.

Prepare an ice bath as on page 225. Blanch the green beans in salted boiling water for 3 to 5 minutes. Transfer to the ice bath. In a large sauté pan with lid, heat the olive oil over medium heat and add the garlic. Sauté until it just begins to brown, about 45 seconds. Quickly add the beans and stock and cover. Shake the pan occasionally so that everything heats evenly. Once the beans are hot, 2 to 3 minutes, remove the lid and add the zest and lemon juice. Season with salt and pepper. Serve hot.

Tempura Mushrooms with Miso Aïoli

SERVES 4 TO 6 AS A SIDE

½ cup all-purpose flour

¼ cup rice flour

¼ cup cornstarch

2 teaspoons baking soda

1 cup sparkling water

4 cups canola oil

4 large portobello mushrooms, stemmed

Kosher salt and freshly ground black pepper

1 cup Miso Aïoli (recipe follows)

THE KEY TO FRYING at home is prep work. Have everything gathered in advance. I prefer a countertop fryer with a temperature gauge, but a heavy-bottomed pot or Dutch oven fitted with a thermometer also works. Once the oil has cooled, you can strain it and refrigerate it for up to 3 or 4 weeks to use again.

In a wide, shallow bowl, combine the flours, cornstarch, and baking soda. Slowly whisk in the sparkling water until smooth. Refrigerate while the oil is heating up.

In a countertop fryer or a heavy-bottomed pot or Dutch oven, bring the canola oil to 350°F. Slice each portobello cap into 4 to 5 pieces at a slight angle. Dredge each slice in the batter until well coated. Hold one corner of one mushroom slice in the oil for 10 seconds, then drop it in. (This keeps the mushroom from sticking to the sides of the fryer.) Repeat with a few more pieces. When you see the edges of the mushrooms turn brown, flip them over to ensure even cooking. Once the batter is crispy on all sides, use a slotted spoon to transfer the mushrooms to a paper towel–lined plate. Repeat with the remaining mushroom slices. Season with salt and pepper and serve with the miso aïoli.

Miso Aïoli MAKES ABOUT 1 CUP

¾ cup mayonnaise

3 tablespoons Garlic Confit (page 224)

3 tablespoons white miso

2 tablespoons freshly squeezed lemon juice

½ teaspoon togarashi, plus more for sprinkling (optional)

Kosher salt and freshly ground black pepper

In a medium bowl, whisk together the mayonnaise, garlic confit, miso, lemon juice, and togarashi, if using. Season with salt and pepper and refrigerate until ready to serve. Sprinkle with togarashi.

Grilled Corn with Parsley Butter and Parmesan SERVES 4 AS A SIDE

5 ears fresh corn, husks and silks removed

2 tablespoons extra-virgin olive oil

Kosher salt and freshly ground black pepper

4 tablespoons Parsley Butter (recipe follows)

2 shallots, thinly sliced

2 teaspoons freshly squeezed lemon juice

3 tablespoons finely grated Parmesan

FOR THIS DISH, do yourself a favor and stop at a farmstand or farmer's market to buy fresh-picked corn at the height of summer–you will thank me. Because the Parmesan is naturally salty, use a light hand when seasoning. And if you don't have a grill, roast the corn in the oven. Parsley butter is great on meat, fish, vegetables, or just spread on bread.

Preheat a grill to medium-high heat.

Brush the ears of corn with the olive oil and season with salt and pepper. Grill the corn, turning frequently, until it is slightly charred with a bit of color on all sides. Remove from the grill and let rest until cool enough to handle. Use a paring knife to shave the corn kernels off the cob, cutting as close to the cob as you can to get the highest yield.

In a large sauté pan set over medium heat, melt the parsley butter. Add the shallots and cook until translucent, 1 to 2 minutes. Add the corn kernels and cook until the mixture is hot and the corn is coated, 4 to 5 minutes. Remove from the heat and add the lemon juice. Season lightly with additional salt and pepper. Place in a serving dish and sprinkle the Parmesan over the top.

Parsley Butter

MAKES 2 STICKS (16 TABLESPOONS)

1 cup flat-leaf parsley leaves

2 sticks (16 tablespoons) unsalted butter, softened

Kosher salt and freshly ground black pepper

Place the parsley in the bowl of a food processor fitted with the metal blade. Cut the butter into 5 or 6 pieces and press down into the parsley with a spoon. Blend until the butter and parsley are whipped together. Scrape the sides of the bowl and pulse a few more times to incorporate. Season with salt and pepper and pulse again to combine. Turn the butter onto a dry surface and divide into 3 to 4 pieces. Place each piece on a sheet of plastic wrap and wrap individually into cylinder shapes.

Store tightly wrapped in the refrigerator for 3 or 4 weeks or in the freezer for up to 3 months.

Chef's Tip: Opt for flat-leaf parsley over curly. Look for big green leaves. Wash the herbs well and use a small salad spinner to dry them. Then pat them dry with a towel before using. The drier the parsley the better.

Roasted Parsnips with Honey and Cayenne

SERVES 4 AS A SIDE

I LOVE THE SWEET, EARTHY flavor of parsnips, especially when I'm fighting off the doldrums of winter. Look for freshly dug parsnips at your local farmstand—they can't be beat. You can also make a variation of this with carrots, turnips, or rutabagas.

Preheat the oven to 350°F.

Trim the ends off of the parsnips. Split in half lengthwise, then cut pieces at an angle so that each piece is about 3 inches long. In a large saucepan, melt the butter over low heat. Whisk in the honey and cayenne. Remove from the heat and add the parsnips. Toss to coat. Season with salt. Transfer the parsnips to a baking sheet in a single layer and roast until tender enough to pierce easily with a cake tester, about 15 minutes.

To serve, transfer the parsnips to a serving dish and pour any excess liquid from the baking sheet over the top.

6 medium parsnips, peeled

3 tablespoons unsalted butter

2 tablespoons honey

¼ teaspoon ground cayenne pepper

Kosher salt

Chef's Tip: A cake tester is a long, thin steel spear that should poke easily through vegetables when they're cooked through. If you meet any resistance, cook the vegetables a little longer.

Cumin-Roasted Sweet Potatoes with Basil Pesto

SERVES 4 AS A SIDE

CUMIN AND THE OTHER SPICES make this dish sing, and the smell of them toasting is amazing. You can use ground spices if you don't have whole ones, though grinding them yourself guarantees freshness. The pesto can be made ahead and goes well with many other dishes.

Preheat the oven to 375°F.

Halve the sweet potatoes lengthwise. Cut the halves in half and then again, for 8 wedges per potato. In a small, dry sauté pan, combine the cumin, mustard seeds, and white peppercorns and toast over low heat until the spices become fragrant. Remove from the heat and allow to cool. Transfer to a spice grinder and pulse until finely ground. In a large bowl, combine the spices with the olive oil. Add the potato wedges, season with salt, and toss to combine. Transfer to a baking sheet and roast for about 25 minutes.

To serve, transfer the cooked potatoes to a serving bowl and distribute the pesto on top, or serve the pesto on the side.

2 medium sweet potatoes, unpeeled

1 teaspoon cumin seeds

1 teaspoon dark mustard seeds

1 teaspoon white peppercorns

3 tablespoons extra-virgin olive oil

Kosher salt

Basil Pesto (recipe follows)

Basil Pesto

MAKES ABOUT 1 CUP

In the bowl of a food processor fitted with the metal blade, add the basil, pine nuts, Parmesan, and garlic and pulse to combine. Leave the machine running and slowly add the olive oil until the mixture is well blended. Season with salt and pepper. Refrigerate in a sealed container for up to 1 week or freeze for up to 1 month.

2½ packed cups fresh basil leaves

3 tablespoons pine nuts, toasted

¼ cup grated Parmesan

3 small cloves garlic, smashed

¾ cup extra-virgin olive oil

Kosher salt and freshly ground black pepper

Winter Squash with Roasted Onions and Red Lentils

SERVES 4 AS A SIDE

1 medium butternut squash

3 tablespoons extra-virgin olive oil

Kosher salt and freshly ground black pepper

1 large red onion

3 tablespoons balsamic vinegar

1 tablespoon honey

1 cup heavy cream

2½ cups vegetable stock or room temperature water

1 small bulb fennel, cored and minced

1 cup red lentils

1 tablespoon finely chopped fresh rosemary leaves

2 tablespoons freshly squeezed lemon juice

1 tablespoon grated lemon zest

2 tablespoons chopped flat-leaf parsley leaves

THIS HEARTY SIDE DISH goes nicely with roasted meats, or it can stand on its own as a main dish. There are plenty of delicious varieties of winter squash, but I often reach for butternut because it's easy to find and to break down. Use a vegetable peeler to peel away the thick skin.

Preheat the oven to 350°F.

Cut off the base and stem of the squash and split it in half lengthwise. Cut off the neck of the squash and set aside. Scoop out and discard the seeds from the belly and arrange the halves cut-sides up on a baking sheet. Brush 1 tablespoon of the olive oil on the squash and season with salt and pepper. Roast for 30 minutes. Remove and allow to cool slightly before scooping the flesh away from the skin.

Meanwhile, slice the onion in half through the root end, then cut into thin wedges without separating the pieces. Arrange the onion in a single layer on one half of a full-size baking sheet. Toss with the balsamic vinegar and honey. Season with salt and pepper. Roast while you peel and dice the neck of the squash. Once the squash neck is diced, remove the baking sheet from the oven and place the squash pieces on the other half of the baking sheet. Toss with 1 tablespoon olive oil. Bake the red onion and squash for an additional 10 minutes. Remove and allow to cool.

In a medium saucepan, combine the cream and ½ cup of the vegetable stock over medium heat. Add the roasted squash flesh. Season with salt and pepper. Simmer until warmed through, 3 to 4 minutes. Remove from the heat and puree with an immersion blender (or in a food processor). Return the puree to the saucepan and keep warm over very low heat.

Heat the remaining 1 tablespoon olive oil in a large sauté pan and sauté the fennel until it begins to color, 2 to 3 minutes. Add the lentils, rosemary, and the remaining 2 cups vegetable stock. Simmer until the lentils are tender, 10 to 12 minutes.

Add the lentil mixture to the baking sheet with the roasted onion and squash cubes. Drizzle with lemon juice, season with salt and pepper, and toss to combine. To serve, spread the squash puree on the bottom of a serving dish and top with the lentil mixture. Scatter on the lemon zest and parsley.

Brussels Sprouts with Bacon and Parmesan

SERVES 4 AS A SIDE

4 cups Brussels sprouts, root ends trimmed and halved

3 tablespoons extra-virgin olive oil

Kosher salt and freshly ground black pepper

6 slices thick-cut bacon, cut into small dice

2 teaspoons sherry vinegar

¼ cup finely grated Parmesan

1 teaspoon grated lemon zest

BRUSSELS SPROUTS HAVE been having their moment. They've become one of the most popular vegetables on restaurant menus in the past few years. When I was a kid, eating them was a punishment (my dad ate them covered in mayonnaise—yuck) so clearly, they've come a long way. I always enjoy seeing how chefs are getting creative with them.

Preheat the oven to 400°F.

Place the Brussels sprouts on a baking sheet. Drizzle with the olive oil and season with salt and pepper. Toss to coat. Arrange the sprouts cut-sides down on the baking sheet. Bake until tender, 25 to 35 minutes. Use a cake tester to test for doneness.

In a sauté pan over medium heat, sauté the bacon until crisp. Reserve about 2 tablespoons of the rendered bacon fat and discard the rest.

Transfer the cooked sprouts to a large bowl. Add the bacon. Heat the reserved fat if it has cooled and add that as well. Add the vinegar. Toss to combine and season with salt and pepper. Transfer to a serving bowl and top with the Parmesan and lemon zest.

Scallion Mashed Potatoes serves 4 to 6 as a side

IT'S HARD TO BEAT good mashed potatoes. Scallion greens add flavor and crunch—once you try these, you might not go back to regular mashed potatoes. Make sure the scallion greens are bright and crisp. I find that a potato ricer or food mill results in a creamier texture, but you can also mix these in a stand mixer.

Preheat the oven to 350°F.

Cut the potatoes into 1-inch pieces and place in a large saucepan. Cover with cold water by about 1 inch and add salt. Bring to a simmer over medium heat. Cook until the potatoes are tender but not falling apart, about 15 minutes. Drain the potatoes and place on a baking sheet. Roast for 5 minutes to dry out the potatoes.

Meanwhile, in a small saucepan, simmer the cream and butter over medium heat until the butter is completely melted.

Remove the potatoes from the oven and use a potato ricer or food mill to puree them, letting them drop into a large bowl. (Alternatively, beat them in a stand mixer fitted with the paddle attachment on medium speed.) Fold in the warm cream and butter mixture until combined. Fold in about half of the scallion greens and season with salt and pepper. Transfer to a serving bowl and sprinkle the remaining scallion greens on top.

4 russet potatoes, peeled

Kosher salt

1 cup heavy cream

1 stick (8 tablespoons) unsalted butter

Green parts of 1 bunch scallions, thinly sliced

Freshly ground black pepper

Chef's Tip: Drying the potatoes thoroughly before ricing them ensures that they will soak up all of the liquid and flavor from the cream and butter. If they're still wet, they risk being watery.

Potato Cake with Chive Crème Fraîche

SERVES 4 AS A SIDE

HERE'S ANOTHER EXAMPLE of how a simple potato can create an amazing dish. Once you learn the technique to this, you'll want to make it all the time since it makes a great side. But my favorite way to eat this is to top it with a fried egg and a little smoked salmon and call it brunch. If you can't find crème fraîche, sour cream works just fine, and feel free to use whatever herb you have on hand, like thyme or sage. This also works as individual portions; just divide the potato mixture evenly into smaller amounts.

In a small bowl, combine the crème fraîche and chive and season with salt and pepper. Refrigerate until ready to use.

Wash the potatoes and place in a saucepan. Cover with cold water by about 1 inch and add salt. Place over high heat until the water is boiling, then reduce the heat to a gentle simmer. Cook until the potatoes are nearly cooked through. (Use a cake tester to check for doneness; you should feel some resistance but still be able to poke through to the center of the potato.)

Drain the potatoes and let cool for 10 minutes. Use paper towels to remove the peels from the potatoes and use a box grater to grate them into a large bowl. Add the onion, egg, flour, and rosemary and season with salt and pepper. Stir to combine.

In an 8-inch nonstick sauté pan, heat the canola oil over medium-high heat. Form the potato mixture into a firm ball and place in the center of the pan. Use a spatula to flatten the ball and press the potato evenly into the pan. Now, press the edges back in toward the center, then press the mixture flat again. (This helps keep the edges from burning and makes the cake an even size.) You should see the oil bubbling around the edges of the potato mixture as it fries. Check for browning by carefully lifting one edge.

When the cake is evenly browned on the bottom, use a large spatula to carefully turn the cake over, trying not to splatter the oil. Again, press in the edges and flatten the cake in the center to hold the shape. Fry the potato cake until it's golden brown on both sides. Transfer to a paper towel–lined plate to drain.

To serve, transfer to a cutting board, quarter, and top with the crème fraîche.

¼ cup crème fraîche

2 tablespoons minced chive

Kosher salt and freshly ground black pepper

2 medium russet potatoes

1 small Spanish onion, minced

1 large egg, beaten

3 tablespoons all-purpose flour

1 teaspoon chopped rosemary leaves

½ cup canola oil

Twice-Baked Potatoes

SERVES 6 TO 8 AS A SIDE

2 cups kosher salt, plus more for seasoning

6 to 8 medium russet potatoes, washed and dried

½ cup heavy cream

1 stick (8 tablespoons) unsalted butter

½ cup sour cream

½ cup grated cheddar cheese

Freshly ground black pepper

Green parts of 1 bunch scallions, thinly sliced

TWICE-BAKED POTATOES are old-school, but they're still around for a reason. Our family loves them for special occasions.

Preheat the oven to 350°F.

Spread the kosher salt onto a baking sheet to create a bed for the potatoes. Use a fork or paring knife to poke 10 to 12 shallow holes in each potato. Place the potatoes on the salt and bake until tender all the way through, about 45 minutes. Remove the potatoes and let cool for about 15 minutes. Slice the top off of each potato lengthwise, exposing the flesh. Scoop out the flesh, leaving the potato skins intact. Transfer the potato flesh to the bowl of a food processor fitted with the metal blade.

Raise the oven temperature to 400°F. In a small saucepan, combine the cream and butter and place over medium heat until the butter is melted. Add the mixture to the food processor along with the sour cream and ¼ cup of the cheddar. Season with salt and pepper. Pulse to combine, scraping down the sides of the bowl as needed. Scoop the filling back into the potato shells and top with the remaining ¼ cup cheddar. Return to the salt-covered baking sheet and bake for 25 minutes. Before serving, sprinkle the scallion greens on top.

Roasted Potatoes with Harissa Aïoli

SERVES 4 AS A SIDE

3 large Yukon gold potatoes

¼ cup extra-virgin olive oil

Kosher salt and freshly ground
black pepper

1¼ cups Harissa Aïoli (recipe
follows)

POTATOES ARE A HUMBLE INGREDIENT, yet they manage to serve as the foundation of some of the most delicious dishes. There is a whole world of potato varieties to explore. This dish can be made with Yukons or nearly any other variety. Don't be shy with the salt, since potatoes can take a lot of it. Harissa is a North African spice mix in the form of a paste or powder.

Preheat the oven to 400°F.

Halve the potatoes lengthwise. Cut each half into 4 to 5 wedges. Place the wedges in a large bowl and toss to coat with the olive oil. Season generously with salt and pepper and transfer to a baking sheet. Roast for 12 minutes. Use a metal spatula to flip the wedges and roast until a cake tester slides through the potatoes easily, about 15 additional minutes. Serve warm with harissa aïoli on the side.

Harissa Aïoli   MAKES 1¼ CUPS

1 cup mayonnaise

3 tablespoons harissa paste

2 tablespoons freshly squeezed
lemon juice

2 teaspoons Garlic Confit
(page 224)

In a medium mixing bowl, stir the ingredients to combine. Cover and refrigerate until ready to use.

Caraway and Cumin Rice with Scallions

SERVES 4 AS A SIDE

USE EITHER BASMATI OR JASMINE rice for this simple side. Follow package instructions for the proper liquid ratio and cooking time. This goes well with the Slow-Roasted Pork Shoulder on page 132 or the Baked Citrus Salmon with Shallot and Dill on page 200.

In a saucepan over medium heat, sauté the onion in the olive oil for 1 to 2 minutes. Add the garlic confit, caraway, turmeric, and cumin, and stir to combine. Add the rice and stir to coat. Add the stock and season with salt and pepper. Bring to a boil and then cover. Reduce the heat to medium-low and simmer until the liquid is absorbed, about 20 minutes. (Check package instructions; times may vary.) Remove the pan from the heat and let it sit, covered, for 10 minutes.

To serve, transfer the rice to a serving dish and top with the scallion greens and lemon zest.

1 small Spanish onion, minced

2 tablespoons extra-virgin olive oil

1 tablespoon Garlic Confit (page 224)

1 teaspoon caraway seeds

1 teaspoon ground turmeric

½ teaspoon ground cumin

2 cups long-grain white rice, such as basmati or jasmine

3 cups vegetable stock

Kosher salt and freshly ground black pepper

Green parts of 3 scallions, thinly sliced

Grated zest of 1 lemon

Potato Gratin with Gruyère and Thyme

SERVES 4 TO 6 AS A SIDE

IF I HAVEN'T MADE IT clear yet, I think potatoes are magic—you can do so much with the humble spud. A gratin like this is the perfect example: It's a showy dish that always impresses a table full of people. Gruyère is a classic pairing with potatoes, but in a pinch you could use cheddar. Pull out the nice-looking baking dish for this one, something with some weight to it, and preferably oval. Be sure to wipe the edges before baking to avoid burnt edges. I like to place the dish on a baking sheet to guard against messy oven spills. You can also prep and bake this a day in advance and refrigerate it overnight. Bring it to room temperature before reheating.

Preheat the oven to 350°F.

In a medium saucepan, combine the cream, garlic, and thyme over medium heat. Simmer for 15 minutes. Remove from the heat and let cool slightly. Strain into a bowl using a fine-mesh strainer and let sit at room temperature.

Drain the potatoes. Using a mandoline, slice the potatoes into thin rounds and add them to the cream. With a spoon, turn the slices in the cream until everything is coated. Spread the butter inside an 8 by 12–inch casserole or baking dish and place it on a baking sheet.

By hand, arrange the potatoes in the dish, starting on the outside edge and working toward the middle, overlapping the slices like shingles. After the first layer, season the potatoes with salt and pepper. Continue creating layers, adding salt and pepper between each one. Pour any remaining cream over the potatoes. It should reach the top layer but not submerge it. Wipe away any cream from the top edges of the dish.

Sprinkle the Gruyère over the top and bake for 25 minutes. Rotate the baking sheet and cook until bubbling and just beginning to brown on top, about 25 additional minutes.

3 cups heavy cream

2 cloves garlic

5 sprigs fresh thyme

5 to 8 russet potatoes (about 3 pounds), peeled and placed in a bowl of cold water

2 tablespoons unsalted butter, softened

Kosher salt and freshly ground black pepper

1 cup grated Gruyère

Ginger Rice with Bok Choy

SERVES 4 AS A SIDE OR A LIGHT MAIN

1 cup brown rice, rinsed

2 cups vegetable stock or room temperature water

1 thumb-size piece ginger, cut into 3 pieces

1 teaspoon kosher salt, plus more for seasoning

2 heads bok choy

3 tablespoons canola oil

1 small carrot, thinly sliced

1 small red bell pepper, seeded and diced

1 shallot, minced

1 tablespoon finely grated peeled fresh ginger

1 tablespoon Garlic Confit (page 224)

Freshly ground black pepper

3 tablespoons soy sauce

Juice of 1 lime

1 tablespoon sriracha

¼ cup Miso Aïoli (page 100)

1 tablespoon sesame seeds, toasted

Green parts of 1 bunch scallions, thinly sliced

I USE GINGER all the time to add a punch of flavor. This dish works as a hearty side, but it can also be a main dish, especially if you top each bowl with a sunny-side up egg (page 227). It's a showstopper when it's plated individually as opposed to family-style. I use brown rice here because it's forgiving to cook and reheats easily. Add or omit any vegetables that you like; if you can't find bok choy, use napa cabbage or kale.

In a medium saucepan, combine the rice, stock, ginger, and the 1 teaspoon salt. Bring to a boil over high heat, then reduce the heat to low and cover. Cook until the liquid is absorbed, 18 to 20 minutes. Remove from the heat and let sit for at least 10 minutes before removing the lid. Drain off any excess liquid and discard the ginger pieces.

Remove the soft green leaves from the bok choy and cut into thin strips. Slice the stems of the bok choy into thin slivers until you get to the core; discard the core. In a large sauté pan, heat the canola oil over medium heat. Add the carrot, bell pepper, and slivered bok choy stems. Sauté until they begin to color. Add the shallot, grated ginger, garlic confit, and bok choy leaves. Cook for an additional 30 seconds, then remove the pan from the heat. Season with salt and pepper.

In a small bowl, whisk together the soy sauce, lime juice, and sriracha.

Spread 2 tablespoons of miso aïoli in four individual serving bowls. Spoon about ½ cup of rice into each bowl. Place a spoonful of sautéed vegetables over the rice and drizzle some of the soy sauce mixture over each portion. Garnish each portion with the toasted sesame seeds and scallion greens.

Leek, Horseradish, and Potato Tart with Pancetta Vinaigrette

MAKES ONE 10-INCH TART, 4 TO 6 SERVINGS

1 leek, halved lengthwise

1 tablespoon unsalted butter, softened

1 large egg

½ cup half-and-half

1 tablespoon prepared horseradish

1 tablespoon grated Parmesan

¼ teaspoon fresh thyme leaves

Kosher salt and freshly ground black pepper

One 10-inch tart shell crust, par-baked and cooled, from Sweet Potato, Broccoli, and Cheddar Quiche (page 35)

1 small Yukon gold potato, peeled

½ cup baby arugula

1 cup Pancetta Vinaigrette (recipe opposite), warm

One ½-inch piece fresh horseradish (optional)

Chef's Tip: Look for fresh horseradish in the produce section, especially at Asian markets. The large root has a tough outer skin, similar to that of ginger, that must be peeled away before grating.

I LIKE THIS COMBO OF leek and potatoes for a fall or winter dish. It can serve as an appetizer or a light meal. For the tart shell, you can use the same recipe used for the quiche on page 35. The crust and the filling can be made a day in advance and assembled just before baking. This recipe takes a bit of a time but it's well worth the effort.

Preheat the oven to 350°F.

Slice the white parts of the leek into thin half-moons. In a medium sauté pan melt the butter over medium heat and add the sliced leeks. Sauté until softened and translucent without letting them color. Set aside to cool.

In a large bowl, whisk together the egg, half-and-half, prepared horseradish, Parmesan, and thyme. Season the custard with salt and pepper and refrigerate.

Arrange the sautéed leeks evenly in the bottom of the par-baked tart shell crust. Use a mandoline to thinly slice the potato and layer the slices over the leeks. Season with salt and pepper. Give the custard a stir, then pour the mixture over the potato slices. The filling should come just below the top edge of the tart shell. Transfer the filled tart to the oven and bake for 12 minutes. Rotate 180 degrees, then continue baking for an additional 15 minutes. Remove and let cool slightly.

To serve, remove the ring around the tart pan and transfer the tart to a cutting board. Slice into 4 to 6 wedges and place on individual serving plates. Top the tart slices with arugula and spoon the warm vinaigrette around and on top of the tart. Finely grate fresh horseradish over the top, if using.

Pancetta Vinaigrette MAKES ABOUT 1 CUP

In a medium sauté pan, sauté the pancetta over medium-high heat until crisp, 8 to 10 minutes. Stir in the shallot and remove from the heat. Drain the fat into a heatproof measuring cup. Reserve ¼ cup and discard the rest. (If the pancetta does not render enough fat, compensate for the difference with a little extra-virgin olive oil.) Transfer the pancetta mixture to a bowl, add the reserved fat, and stir in the sherry vinegar. Season with salt and pepper and keep warm.

1 cup diced pancetta

1 large shallot, diced

2 tablespoons sherry vinegar

Kosher salt and freshly ground black pepper

Ricotta-Filled Eggplant with Tomato Sauce and Parmesan

SERVES 4 AS A SIDE OR A MAIN

1 large eggplant

¼ cup extra-virgin olive oil

Kosher salt and freshly ground black pepper

1 cup ricotta cheese

½ cup grated Parmesan

1 tablespoon Garlic Confit (page 224)

12 large basil leaves, torn into small pieces

1 teaspoon chopped fresh oregano leaves, plus more leaves for garnish

3 cups Tomato Sauce (page 226)

THIS IS ONE OF my favorite ways to eat eggplant and it's easy to make in advance and pop in the oven before serving. Look for a large eggplant. If you can only find small ones, think of getting two so you have enough slices to make the rolls. I call for fresh tomato sauce here (see recipe, page 226) but a good jarred sauce will work. To vary the dish, replace the herbs with pesto or grill the eggplant slices rather than bake them. Either way, this dish is full of flavor.

Preheat the oven to 325°F.

Remove the stem end from the eggplant and cut lengthwise into 8 thin slices. Brush each slice with some of the olive oil and season with salt and pepper. Arrange the slices in a single layer on a baking sheet and roast for 7 minutes. Flip the slices over and roast for an additional 4 minutes. Remove and let cool to room temperature. Raise the oven temperature to 350°F.

In a medium bowl, stir together the ricotta, ¼ cup of the Parmesan, the garlic confit, basil, and chopped oregano. Season with salt and pepper. Spoon about 2 tablespoons of the ricotta mixture onto the wider end of each eggplant slice and roll each slice into a cylinder.

Spread 1½ cups tomato sauce in the bottom of a medium baking dish. Place the stuffed eggplant rolls in the dish seam-sides down, leaving a little space between them. Spoon the remaining sauce around the eggplant rolls and top with the remaining ¼ cup Parmesan. Bake until the sauce is gently bubbling around the edges, about 35 minutes. Remove from the oven and drizzle with the remaining olive oil before serving. Garnish with the whole oregano leaves.

Creamy Polenta with Roasted Mushrooms and Sage SERVES 4 TO 6 AS A SIDE

POLENTA IS ONE OF my favorite things to eat in colder months. It's deeply comforting. Avoid instant polenta, as the texture is just too mushy. My favorite polenta brands are Anson Mills and Maine Grains. They both ship and put care into their product. Be sure to read the packaging for cooking instructions as they vary depending on the grind. Take your time cooking the polenta and always use a heavy-bottomed pot to keep it from burning. If you don't have mascarpone, substitute sour cream or crème fraîche.

In a heavy-bottomed pot or Dutch oven, melt the butter over medium heat. Sauté the onion until it begins to soften, 3 to 5 minutes. Add the stock and milk and bring to a boil. Reduce to a simmer and then add the polenta in a thin stream while whisking briskly to avoid lumps. Bring the mixture back to a boil and season with salt and pepper. Reduce the heat to medium-low; the mixture should be barely bubbling. Cook according to package instructions until thick and creamy (usually about 45 minutes), stirring often to keep the mixture from sticking. If the polenta becomes thick but still tastes raw, add more stock. Remove from the heat and stir in the Parmesan and mascarpone.

Meanwhile, preheat the oven to 350°F.

On a baking sheet, toss the mushrooms with the olive oil and season with salt and pepper. Roast for 20 minutes. Remove the baking sheet and carefully pour any liquid that has collected in the bottom into a small bowl and set aside. Return the baking sheet to the oven and roast the mushrooms for 10 additional minutes.

Meanwhile, pour the canola oil into a small, high-sided saucepan and heat to 350°F. Add the sage leaves and fry until crisp but still green in color, 1 to 2 minutes. With a slotted spoon, transfer them to a paper towel–lined plate to drain. Season with a little salt.

When ready to serve, transfer the polenta to a serving dish and pour the mushroom liquid over the top. Top with the roasted mushrooms and fried sage.

2 tablespoons unsalted butter

1 small Spanish onion, minced

2 cups vegetable stock, plus more as needed

2 cups whole milk

1 cup medium-grind polenta

Kosher salt and freshly ground black pepper

¼ cup grated Parmesan

¼ cup mascarpone

8 ounces cremini mushrooms, stemmed and quartered

2 tablespoons extra-virgin olive oil

½ cup canola oil

12 large sage leaves

Chapter 7
Feeding a Crowd

Getting a group around the table, and then filling that table with food, can seem daunting, but it doesn't have to be. Throughout the book, my message is the same: Prepare in advance. And keep the menu small and manageable. I've learned the hard way that all you need are a few standout dishes, not a bunch of mediocre ones. A well-made lasagna served alongside a Caesar salad is a great meal. Don't overthink it.

Also, ask for help. Whoever is joining you won't mind pitching in. Have them roll out the pizza dough and put the toppings out so everyone can choose their own. Or have them warm up the sauce. The more you can do ahead of time, especially when it comes to shopping, the easier and more fun the gathering will be.

Most of these meals are casual. Set the Sheet Tray Pizza (page 192) or the Roasted Salt and Pepper Chicken with Pan-Fried Potatoes (page 202) on the counter or buffet and let everyone help themselves. The one exception is Grilled Ribeye Steaks with Black Pepper Butter (page 196), because those are best served as a seated meal, preferably with baked potatoes and asparagus. Whether fancy or homey, these dishes are meant to be shared. Feel free to mix and match them with others throughout the cookbook to put together a simple and easy-to-execute menu.

Sheet Tray Pizza

MAKES 2 LARGE PIZZAS; SERVES 6 TO 10

HERE'S YOUR CHANCE to get the entire family into the kitchen together. This is a stand-around-the-counter-and-eat-off-paper-plates kind of meal, great for a time when people are coming and going. You can make the dough in advance and freeze it, then let it thaw in the refrigerator the night before cooking. I usually offer a couple of simple toppings, but you can also get creative here. Ricotta and honey? Why not. You can also put out fresh herbs and chili flakes for topping the slices after baking. But dough, sauce, and cheese are a solid start. Oven temperatures vary, so keep an eye on the pizza and cook it as long as necessary to ensure the crust is crisp.

To make the dough, in the bowl of a stand mixer fitted with the dough hook, combine the water and yeast and let sit for 20 minutes. Add the salt and ½ cup of the olive oil and turn on the mixer to medium speed. Add 6 cups of the all-purpose flour and the whole wheat flour 1 cup at a time, mixing to combine between additions. Once all of the flour is added, continue mixing until the dough forms a ball. It should feel moist but not sticky; add 1 to 2 more tablespoons all-purpose flour if it isn't coming together. Transfer the dough to a clean, dry surface and knead by hand for a few minutes until the dough is smooth and pliable. Place in a bowl coated with olive oil and cover. Let proof in a warm place until doubled in size, about 45 minutes.

Divide the dough into two equal balls. Dust a work surface with the remaining ½ cup all-purpose flour and roll each ball into a long rectangle. Brush two 13 by 18–inch baking sheets with the remaining ¼ cup olive oil. Transfer the dough to the baking sheets, pushing the dough into the surface and corners; it doesn't have to fit perfectly, but the thickness should be even.

To top and bake the pizzas, preheat the oven to 450°F.

Divide the sauce evenly, spreading across both rectangles of dough. On one pizza, arrange the basil leaves on top of the sauce and top with half of the grated mozzarella cheese and the Parmesan. On the other pizza, spread the remaining mozzarella. Top with the pepperoni slices and drizzle the garlic confit over the top. Bake both pizzas for 10 minutes. Rotate the baking sheets and bake for an additional 15 minutes. Remove from the oven and allow to cool for 5 minutes before slicing and serving.

DOUGH

2½ cups warm water

2 tablespoons active dry yeast

2 tablespoons kosher salt

¾ cup extra-virgin olive oil, plus more for bowl

6½ cups all-purpose flour, plus more for dusting and as needed

2 cups whole wheat flour

TOPPINGS

4 cups Tomato Sauce (page 226)

12 large basil leaves

3 cups grated full-fat mozzarella

½ cup grated Parmesan

2 cups sliced pepperoni

3 tablespoons Garlic Confit (page 224)

Grilled Ribeye Steaks with Black Pepper Butter   SERVES 6 TO 8

2 tablespoons Garlic Confit
   (page 224)

½ cup extra-virgin olive oil

Four 12-ounce ribeye steaks

Kosher salt and freshly ground
   black pepper

4 tablespoons Black Pepper
   Butter (recipe follows)

Sea salt

RIBEYE STEAKS ARE celebratory, and their size alone makes them suitable for a group. They also pack a ton of flavor, especially when grilled over wood or charcoal. Keep an eye on these while they are cooking, as their thickness and desired doneness determine the cooking time. Definitely use a meat thermometer to gauge temperature. I call for black pepper butter here but you could also use the Parsley Butter from page 164. Serve these with Twice-Baked Potatoes (page 174), Grilled Asparagus with Orange and Watercress (page 148), plus a big salad for the perfect outdoor feast.

Combine the garlic confit and oil in a small bowl and mash with a fork. Rub the mixture onto the steaks. Place the steaks on a platter and refrigerate for 1 hour.

Build a fire in a wood or charcoal grill, or heat a gas grill to medium-high.

Season the steaks generously with salt and pepper. Place the steaks on the hot grill and grill without moving for 3 to 4 minutes. If the fire flares up, move the steaks so they don't burn. Rotate the steaks a quarter-turn and cook for 2 to 3 minutes. Rotate another quarter-turn and cook for another 2 to 3 minutes. Flip the steaks and repeat the rotation. Use a meat thermometer to check the temperature. For medium-rare, the internal temperature should be 120°F. If you prefer medium, rotate the meat and cook for another 2 to 3 minutes.

When the steaks are cooked to the desired temperature, place 1 tablespoon black pepper butter on top of each and let them sit on the grill until the butter is melted. Transfer the steaks from the grill to a cutting board and let rest for 10 minutes. To serve, slice the steaks against the grain and season the slices with sea salt.

Black Pepper Butter

MAKES 2 STICKS (16 TABLESPOONS)

In a dry sauté pan over medium heat, toast the ground black pepper until fragrant, about 45 seconds.

Transfer to the bowl of a food processor fitted with the metal blade and add the remaining ingredients. Puree the mixture until it's well incorporated. Scrape down the sides of the bowl and pulse to combine.

Place a square of parchment paper or plastic wrap on a flat surface. Scrape the butter mixture onto the paper or plastic and use the paper or plastic to roll it into a cylinder.

Refrigerate for at least 30 minutes before using. Tightly wrapped butter will keep in the refrigerator for 2 to 3 weeks or in the freezer for 3 to 4 months. Allow frozen butter to thaw in the refrigerator for 2 hours before using.

1 teaspoon freshly ground
   black pepper

2 sticks (16 tablespoons)
   unsalted butter, room
   temperature

2 tablespoons grated Parmesan

1 tablespoon Garlic Confit
   (page 224)

½ teaspoon Aleppo pepper

Baked Citrus Salmon with Shallot and Dill

SERVES 4, OR DOUBLE OR TRIPLE TO FEED 8 TO 12

EVERYONE NEEDS A GOOD weeknight salmon recipe and this is mine—simple, quick, and delicious. It's also a crowd-pleaser and is easily doubled or tripled for a large group. Cook the salmon with the skin on—this keeps the salmon juicy—but remove it before serving. And be sure to watch your cooking time, as thicker pieces might take a little longer. Make a meal of this dish by pairing it with the Winter Squash with Roasted Onions and Red Lentils (page 168) and Roasted Broccoli Rabe with Calabrian Chili and Lemon (page 156).

Preheat the oven to 325°F.

Brush a baking sheet with the canola oil and place the salmon fillets skin-sides down on the sheet. Season with salt and pepper. In a small bowl, combine the shallot with the orange zest and juice and the olive oil. Rub the mixture into the fillets. Roast for 8 minutes.

Meanwhile, in a small bowl, combine the orange segments, lemon juice, and dill.

Remove the salmon from the oven and use a thin spatula to remove the skins. Transfer the fillets to a serving dish. Spoon the orange segment mixture over the fillets and serve.

1 tablespoon canola oil

Four 7-ounce salmon fillets, skin on

Kosher salt and freshly ground black pepper

1 large shallot, minced

1 navel or blood orange, zested, then supremed (see Chef's Tip on page 122) and juices reserved

2 tablespoons extra-virgin olive oil

1 teaspoon freshly squeezed lemon juice

1 tablespoon chopped fresh dill

Chef's Tip: Shopping for salmon can be overwhelming because there are so many options. Wild-caught king and sockeye salmon are great choices, but pricey. There is also quality farmed salmon, and there are even frozen options. Do a little taste-testing to determine your personal preference.

Roasted Salt and Pepper Chicken with Pan-Fried Potatoes
SERVES 6 TO 8

8 skin-on, bone-in whole chicken legs

1 cup canola oil

Kosher salt and freshly ground black pepper

4 russet potatoes, peeled

Hot sauce for serving, preferably green Tabasco or Cholula

THIS RECIPE BRINGS ME BACK to the days when I was first living on my own and had limited funds. If you work in the restaurant business, sometimes the best meal of your week is a staff meal provided by the restaurant. Young chefs are kind of like starving artists: Passion fuels what they do, but it's hard to support yourself when you're starting out. I learned early on that whole chicken legs are an affordable cut of protein that offer big flavor. I would buy a package of chicken legs, a couple of potatoes, and some hot sauce, and that would be my big meal of the week. This recipe still holds and makes my family happy—we're fans of eating with our hands. Make sure the skin is intact on the chicken legs. The crisp skin is the best part.

Preheat the oven to 300°F.

Place one leg on a cutting board skin-side down. Cut the thigh from the leg by slicing through the joint. (There is a thin line of fat at the joint; slice down and through it and the pieces should separate easily.) If there are large pieces of skin hanging over the chicken pieces, trim them off, but be sure that the meat is still completely covered by skin. Repeat with the remaining legs.

In a large bowl, toss the chicken with ¼ cup of the canola oil. Generously season the chicken with salt and pepper. Arrange the chicken on a rimmed baking sheet skin-sides up. Roast for 25 minutes. Rotate the baking sheet, then raise the oven temperature to 425°F. Roast until the skin is really crisp, about 12 additional minutes. Carefully remove the baking sheet from the oven; there will be hot fat in the bottom of the pan. Pour the fat from the baking sheet into a large sauté pan.

Halve the potatoes lengthwise, then cut into ½-inch pieces. Add the remaining ¼ cup canola oil to the pan with the chicken fat and place over medium-high heat. Once hot, add the potatoes to the pan and fry until they are browned on both sides and cooked through, 10 to 12 minutes. Taste and season with salt and pepper. Serve the chicken with the potatoes and pass the hot sauce on the side.

Grilled Flank Steak with Chimichurri

SERVES 6 TO 8

3 cloves garlic, minced

3 tablespoons extra-virgin
  olive oil

¼ teaspoon smoked paprika

¼ teaspoon freshly ground
  black pepper

One 3-pound flank steak or
  2 smaller ones

Kosher salt

Sea salt

1 cup Chimichurri (recipe
  follows)

FLANK STEAK IS AN often-undervalued cut of meat. It's full of flavor and great for sharing. Typically, the center of a flank steak is thicker, so the thinner ends cook faster. This is actually a plus: If you get the center of the steak to 120°F, you'll have enough medium-rare and medium pieces to satisfy a crowd. This cut also loves a good rub of garlic and spices and can be cooked on a grill or in a cast-iron pan. If you can't find a large flank steak, look for two smaller ones. Trim off any large pieces of fat and you're ready to go.

Preheat a grill to medium-high heat.

In a small bowl, combine the garlic, olive oil, paprika, and black pepper. Pat the steak dry, then rub the garlic mixture all over both sides. Season liberally with kosher salt.

Place the steak on the hot grill. Sear for 4 to 5 minutes, rotating it once or twice. Flip the steak and continue cooking and rotating for another 4 to 5 minutes. Both sides should have an even char. Test the internal temperature and continue cooking until the steak reaches the desired doneness.

Let the steak rest for about 10 minutes. Slice the meat against the grain and season with sea salt. Serve the chimichurri on the side.

Chimichurri MAKES ABOUT 1 CUP

4 teaspoons Garlic Confit
  (page 224)

½ cup extra-virgin olive oil

1 small shallot, minced

1 Fresno pepper, seeded and
  minced

¼ cup red wine vinegar

½ cup chopped flat-leaf parsley
  leaves

¼ cup chopped cilantro leaves

¼ cup chopped fresh oregano
  leaves

Kosher salt and freshly ground
  black pepper

In a medium bowl, mash the garlic confit with the olive oil to form a paste. Stir in the remaining ingredients and season with salt and pepper. Cover and refrigerate for up to 4 days.

Chef's Tip: Chimichurri is an herbal Argentinian sauce that traditionally is served with steak, but it also complements seafood and vegetables. Be sure your herbs are clean and dry before chopping.

Roasted Vegetable Lasagna SERVES 6 TO 8

I KNOW I'M IN the minority, but I'm not a huge fan of lasagna. What I do enjoy is making it for my family. My sister Mary served lasagna often, and I always think of her while I'm making it. Mary used canned tomato sauce and inexpensive ricotta, but that didn't matter—for Mary, lasagna was about gathering family for a feast. Mary loved sauce and cheese, but not vegetables, but I incorporate vegetables for a healthy-ish version. If you don't have fresh oregano, use dried oregano instead. Lasagna can be assembled in advance and refrigerated overnight before baking. It also makes great leftovers.

Bring a large pot of salted water to a boil. Cook the lasagna noodles until slightly tender (about 2 to 3 minutes less than the package instructions). Drain the noodles, then arrange them flat on a baking sheet and rub with a little olive oil to prevent them from sticking.

In a large sauté pan, heat the canola oil over medium-high heat. Add the eggplant and sauté until it begins to color, 3 to 4 minutes. Use a slotted spoon to transfer the eggplant to a plate, leaving the oil in the pan. Add the onion and red pepper to the pan and cook until they begin to soften, 4 to 5 minutes. Add the zucchini and garlic. Sauté until all of the vegetables have softened, another 3 to 4 minutes. Stir in the tomatoes and remove the pan from the heat. Pour off any excess oil from the pan, then stir in the eggplant. Tear the basil leaves and stir them into the vegetables. Season the mixture with salt and pepper. Let the mixture cool to room temperature.

In a medium bowl, stir together the ricotta, eggs, and oregano. Season with the 1 teaspoon salt and the ½ teaspoon pepper.

Preheat the oven to 350°F.

Brush a 9 by 13–inch baking dish with the 1 tablespoon olive oil. (See next spread for photos.) Spread 1 cup of the tomato sauce into the bottom of the dish, followed by a layer of cooked noodles. Spread one-third of the ricotta mixture over the noodles, then add about one-third of the vegetables. Repeat two more times with the sauce, noodles, ricotta, and vegetables. Top with the remaining ½ cup tomato sauce and layer the sliced mozzarella over the top. Sprinkle the Parmesan on top and season with salt and pepper. Place the baking dish on a baking sheet to prevent messy spills. Bake the lasagna for 30 minutes. Rotate the pan and bake for an additional 20 minutes. Remove from the oven and let cool for 20 minutes before serving.

1 teaspoon kosher salt, plus more for pasta water and to taste

1 pound dried lasagna noodles

1 tablespoon extra-virgin olive oil, plus more for noodles

¼ cup canola oil

1 small eggplant, diced

1 small red onion, diced

1 small red bell pepper, seeded and diced

1 small zucchini, diced

4 cloves garlic, chopped

1 pint medley cherry tomatoes, halved

12 large basil leaves

½ teaspoon freshly ground black pepper, plus more to taste

16 ounces whole milk ricotta

2 large eggs

2 tablespoons chopped fresh oregano leaves

3½ cups Tomato Sauce (page 226)

1 pound fresh mozzarella, thinly sliced

½ cup grated Parmesan

Tacos for a Crowd SERVES 6 TO 8

1 to 2 tablespoons canola oil

16 corn or flour tortillas

Slow-Roasted Pork Shoulder (page 132)

Simple Black Beans (page 230)

Caraway and Cumin Rice with Scallions (page 177)

Grilled shrimp from Grilled Shrimp with Papaya and Avocado (page 92)

2 limes, cut into wedges

½ cup cilantro leaves

2 jalapeño peppers, thinly sliced

2 Fresno peppers, thinly sliced

Hot sauce for serving

1 cup Lime Crema (recipe opposite)

1½ cups Pico de Gallo (recipe opposite)

2 cups Guacamole (recipe opposite)

IN OUR HOUSE, EVERYONE loves taco night. Who doesn't relish the opportunity to shove a lot of deliciousness into a handheld tortilla? Plus, everyone has a chance to combine their favorites. We frequently have taco parties when we're watching football on Sundays. We make everything in advance and then put out all of the fixings and let everyone have at it. The recipe below pulls from a lot of other recipes in the book, but you can sub in whatever you have on hand, like leftover slices of the Grilled Flank Steak on page 204. I lightly toast tortillas in a pan with just a smear of oil, but if you're cooking for a crowd, it's easier to wrap 6 to 8 tortillas in foil and warm them in a low-temperature oven. I prefer the taste of corn tortillas, though flour tortillas are a little more sturdy. I've included recipes for crema, pico de gallo, and guacamole opposite. You can purchase those if you prefer, but they're very easy to make yourself. Make sure the avocados for the guacamole are ripe and slightly soft. I buy mine a few days before I'm going to use them.

Brush a small amount of oil on the bottom of a sauté pan set over medium-high heat. Place a tortilla in the pan until warmed through, 30 seconds to 1 minute. Flip the tortilla and let sit for another 30 seconds. Transfer the tortilla to a flatweave kitchen towel and wrap to keep warm. Repeat with the remaining tortillas and oil. (Alternatively, wrap 6 to 8 tortillas in foil and place in an oven at 250°F until warmed through, 8 to 10 minutes. Keep warm in a kitchen towel.)

Reheat the pork, beans, rice, and shrimp and place each of them on a separate platter. Set out the tortillas. Put the lime wedges, cilantro, jalapeños, and Fresnos in separate bowls, and set out the hot sauce, lime crema, pico de gallo, and guacamole. Have everyone help themselves.

Lime Crema MAKES 1 CUP

1 tablespoon Garlic Confit (page 224)
Finely grated zest and juice of 1 lime
1 cup sour cream
Kosher salt and freshly ground black pepper

In a medium bowl, mash the garlic confit with the lime juice. Stir in the zest and sour cream. Season with salt and pepper and refrigerate until using.

Pico de Gallo MAKES 1½ CUPS

2 large red tomatoes, cored and diced, juices reserved
1 small jalapeño or Fresno pepper, seeded and minced
1 small red onion, diced
3 tablespoons freshly squeezed lime juice
3 tablespoons roughly chopped cilantro leaves
Kosher salt and freshly ground black pepper

In a medium bowl, combine the tomatoes, jalapeño, onion, lime juice, and cilantro. Season with salt and pepper and refrigerate until ready to use.

Guacamole MAKES ABOUT 2 CUPS

4 ripe avocados
¼ cup freshly squeezed lime juice
1 small red onion, minced
1 large clove garlic, finely grated
2 tablespoons chopped cilantro leaves
1 tablespoon red Tabasco sauce
¼ teaspoon ground cumin
Kosher salt and freshly ground black pepper

Split the avocados in half and remove the pits. Scoop the flesh into a large bowl and add the lime juice. Mash with a fork or spoon. Add the remaining ingredients and season to taste with salt and pepper. Place a piece of plastic wrap directly on the surface of the guacamole so that the entire surface is covered (this will keep it from oxidizing). Refrigerate until ready to use.

Chapter 8
Desserts

Desserts are strongly nostalgic. With just a flavor or smell, they bring you right back to childhood. Nana's Molasses Cookies (page 216) are my grandmother's recipe (or close to it, since she never wrote it down) and a trip to her house wasn't complete without one. She lived to be over 100 and lived in the same house for more than sixty years. I ate a lot of cookies there into my forties, and the smell of them baking brings me right back to her.

My wife, Lisa, is a pastry chef and has always been in charge of desserts at our house. I've gotten a little spoiled having someone who can whip up elaborate confections at home that are absolutely delicious. For this chapter, we teamed up to give you a few favorites that are easy to master. At home, simpler is better, so we kept these recipes low-key. Don't skip dessert!

Nana's Molasses Cookies   MAKES ABOUT 24 COOKIES

MY GRANDMOTHER BERTINE lived to 101 and spent all her life in York, Maine. She made the best molasses cookies but never wrote down her recipe. Eating them now isn't quite the same as eating them in her kitchen next to the old woodstove, but their smell and flavor bring me right back to her home. Every time I make these, I bore my kids with a story about visiting my grandmother—that's what nostalgia will do. These are also great crumbled over vanilla ice cream.

Preheat the oven to 350°F.

In the bowl of a stand mixer fitted with the paddle attachment or in a bowl with a wooden spoon, beat the egg, butter, molasses, vanilla, and sugar. In a separate bowl, sift together the flour, salt, baking soda, baking powder, ginger, and cloves. Add the dry ingredients to the wet ingredients and mix just until a dough forms.

Form 1-inch balls of dough, rolling them between your palms, and place them on ungreased baking sheets with about 2 inches between them. Press on each ball lightly with your palm to flatten. Bake until golden brown at the edges and cooked through, 10 to 15 minutes. Cool on the pans on a rack.

1 large egg

1 stick (8 tablespoons) unsalted butter, softened

1 cup mild molasses

1 teaspoon pure vanilla extract

½ cup granulated sugar

3 cups all-purpose flour

½ teaspoon kosher salt

1 teaspoon baking soda

2 teaspoons baking powder

1 teaspoon ground ginger

¼ teaspoon ground cloves

Lemon Pound Cake with Strawberries and Whipped Cream SERVES 4

CAKE

1½ sticks (12 tablespoons) unsalted butter, softened, plus more for the pan

1½ cups sifted cake flour, plus more for the pan

3 tablespoons whole milk

1 teaspoon pure vanilla extract

1 tablespoon freshly squeezed lemon juice

2 large eggs

¾ cup granulated sugar

¾ teaspoon baking powder

¼ teaspoon kosher salt

Finely grated zest of 1 lemon

BERRIES

1 quart strawberries, hulled and sliced

¼ cup granulated sugar

WHIPPED CREAM

2 cups heavy cream

¼ cup confectioners' sugar

2 teaspoons pure vanilla extract

THIS SIMPLE DESSERT is great for the summertime when berries are abundant. You won't need the entire pound cake to make four servings, so I slice and freeze the leftover cake. Jeremy likes to toast and butter the slices lightly and enjoy them for breakfast. For the berries, use local if you can, or even better, pick your own. *—Lisa Sewall*

To make the cake, preheat the oven to 350°F. Butter and flour an 8 by 4–inch loaf pan and set aside.

In a medium bowl, whisk together the milk, vanilla, lemon juice, and eggs.

In the bowl of a stand mixer fitted with the paddle attachment, combine the 1½ cups cake flour, sugar, baking powder, salt, and lemon zest, and mix on low speed for 30 seconds to combine. Add the 1½ sticks butter and half of the egg mixture and mix on low speed until the mixture starts to form a batter. Increase the speed to medium and mix until light and fluffy, 1 additional minute.

Scrape down the sides of the bowl and add the remaining egg mixture in 2 batches, mixing for 30 seconds between additions. Scrape the batter into the prepared loaf pan and smooth the surface. Bake until the outside is golden brown and a cake tester inserted in the center comes out clean, about 45 minutes.

Remove the cake from the oven and let it cool in the pan for 30 minutes. Unmold the cake onto a wire rack and allow to cool completely, 1 to 2 hours.

For the berries, in a small bowl combine the berries and sugar and let sit at room temperature for about 30 minutes before serving.

For the whipped cream, in a large bowl, using a whisk or an electric mixer, beat the cream, confectioners' sugar, and vanilla to soft peaks. Refrigerate until ready to use.

To serve, cut 4 slices from the pound cake and warm them in a low oven or a microwave. Place each slice in a shallow individual serving bowl. Spoon the berries and some of their juices over each slice and top with whipped cream.

Stored in an airtight container or wrapped tightly in plastic wrap, any leftover cake will keep for 3 to 4 days at room temperature and up to 1 week in the refrigerator. It will keep for 1 month in the freezer.

Chocolate Pots de Crème   SERVES 4

THIS FANCY VERSION OF chocolate pudding is a crowd favorite and easy to master. The custards will last for a few days in the refrigerator, so feel free to make them ahead of time. To change things up, you can use milk chocolate rather than semi-sweet. If you want to gild the lily, top these with the whipped cream from the previous recipe just before serving. —*Lisa Sewall*

4 ounces semi-sweet chocolate

¾ cup heavy cream

4 egg yolks

¼ cup plus 2 tablespoons granulated sugar

2 teaspoons cocoa powder

¼ teaspoon kosher salt

¾ cup whole milk

1½ teaspoons pure vanilla extract

Preheat the oven to 325°F.

Finely chop the chocolate and place in a heatproof bowl. Place the cream in a small saucepan over medium-high heat. As soon as it comes to a simmer, remove from the heat and pour the scalded cream over the chocolate. Cover the bowl with plastic wrap and let sit for 10 minutes. Whisk the chocolate mixture completely smooth.

In another bowl, whisk the egg yolks. Add the chocolate mixture to the eggs in small amounts, whisking between additions. Whisk until the chocolate is fully incorporated.

In a medium saucepan, whisk together the sugar, cocoa powder, and salt and add the milk in a thin stream while whisking constantly. Smooth out any lumps. Cook over medium heat, stirring frequently, until the mixture begins to steam.

Add half of the hot milk mixture to the egg mixture in a thin stream while whisking constantly to avoid cooking the eggs. Once the first half is incorporated, whisk in the remaining milk mixture. Stir in the vanilla.

Strain the mixture through a fine-mesh strainer into four 4-ounce ramekins. (They should be about three-quarters full.) Place the ramekins in a high-sided pan and fill the pan with water that reaches halfway up the sides of the ramekins.

Transfer the pan to the oven and bake until the edges of the custards are set and the middles are still slightly wobbly, about 30 minutes. Remove the pan from the oven and allow the ramekins to cool in the water for 15 minutes. Carefully remove the ramekins from the water and allow to cool at room temperature for another 30 minutes. Cover the custards and refrigerate for at least 3 hours and up to 4 days.

Chapter 9
How To

As in most things in life, repetition is the key to success in cooking. When you're just starting out you're bound to make mistakes. And that is absolutely okay, because mistakes help us learn, especially when it comes to cooking.

Give yourself the best chance at success by being prepared. Have all of your ingredients and equipment out before you start cooking. Salt your water. Check for doneness frequently at the end of the allotted cooking time. Set a timer. Use a cake tester to check for doneness. Use a meat thermometer. All of these practices will become natural in time.

The techniques for cooking eggs, pasta, and beans and blanching vegetables are easy. They are also great building blocks to becoming a really good home cook. Experienced chefs have a deep respect for those who can cook eggs or blanch vegetables properly. You can always cook things a little more but never a little less. Be patient with yourself and keep practicing.

How to Make Garlic Confit

I use garlic confit frequently throughout this book because it adds rich garlic flavor instead of the intense bitter taste of raw garlic. To confit something is to cook and preserve it in oil, and the garlic infuses the oil with deep flavor while the oil softens the cloves in return. Use a cake tester to test for doneness. It should easily pierce the cooked cloves. I like to make a batch or two of garlic confit and store it in the refrigerator; it will keep for up to 3 weeks.

Garlic Confit MAKES 1 CUP

2 heads garlic (24 to 30 cloves)
1 cup extra-virgin olive oil

Separate the garlic cloves. Use a paring knife to peel off the skin and trim the root ends off of each clove. Place the cloves in a small saucepan and add the olive oil. It should cover the garlic. Place the saucepan over medium-low heat. When the oil begins to bubble, reduce the heat to low and simmer until the cloves begin to brown very lightly, about 10 minutes. Test a few cloves with a cake tester. When the cloves are soft, remove the pan from the heat and let the cloves cool in the oil. Pour the garlic cloves and the oil into a blender and blend until smooth. Store the garlic confit and oil in an airtight container in the refrigerator.

How to Roast Peppers

Roasted peppers pack a punch of flavor and they're easy to make at home. I use this method to roast red and yellow bell peppers, but it also works with jalapeños and other varieties.

Roasted Red Peppers MAKES ABOUT 1 CUP

1 tablespoon extra-virgin olive oil
2 red bell peppers

Preheat the oven to 400°F.

Rub the olive oil all over the outside of the peppers and place them on a baking sheet. Roast for 10 minutes. Use tongs to flip the peppers, then roast for 5 additional minutes. Remove them from the oven and place in a bowl and cover the bowl tightly with plastic wrap. Let the peppers steam in the bowl for 15 minutes; they should be very pliable. Remove the peppers and use a paring knife to scrape the outer skin from each pepper. Halve and seed the peppers. Cut the flesh as desired (strips, diced, or minced) and refrigerate in an airtight container for up to 3 days.

How to Make Basic Pickled Beets

I like to use red and golden beets because the contrasting colors are pretty together, but they need to be cooked and stored separately—otherwise the red beets will stain the golden beets. Scrub the beets well before cooking them. Your trusty cake tester is a great tool to check the doneness of the beets. If it slides through with little resistance, the beets are done.

1 bunch small or medium red or golden beets (4 to 6 beets),
    greens removed
1 cup granulated sugar
1 cup white wine vinegar or cider vinegar
1 tablespoon kosher salt
1 teaspoon fennel seeds
1 teaspoon coriander seeds
1 teaspoon yellow mustard seeds

Place the beets in a medium stockpot, add cold water to cover (about 6 cups), and add the remaining ingredients. Bring to a gentle simmer over medium-high heat. Simmer until the beets are cooked through but not mushy—a little al dente in the center—20 to 30 minutes. Remove the pot from the heat and let the beets cool in the liquid. Once the beets are cool, use a slotted spoon to remove them. Strain the liquid through a fine-mesh strainer and reserve. Remove the beet skins by rubbing them with a paper towel; the skins should slide right off. Dice the beets and transfer to an airtight container. Pour enough strained liquid over the beets to cover them completely. Store in the refrigerator for up to 3 weeks.

How to Blanch Vegetables

Different types of cooking methods work best with different vegetables. I like to sauté leafy greens like spinach, Swiss chard, and kale in olive oil with lemon and garlic. Most sturdier vegetables respond well to blanching, which means boiling them briefly and then transferring them to an ice bath, which stops them from cooking further and helps them retain their color and texture. Sometimes that's all the cooking they need, and sometimes the vegetables are then finished with another method. (If the vegetables are going to be blanched and then finished before serving, you can usually skip the ice bath.)

To blanch vegetables, you need a large stockpot or saucepan, a slotted spoon for removing the vegetables from the boiling water, and an ice bath (a bowl of ice water).

Prepare an ice bath with a one-to-one ratio of cold water to ice. Fill a medium or large stockpot or saucepan with water. For every 1 quart water, add 1 tablespoon kosher salt. Bring the water to a rolling boil and add the vegetables. Do not add too many vegetables at once; you want the water to start boiling again quickly. Work in batches if necessary. Most vegetables will take 2 to 4 minutes to be cooked properly, though of course that timing depends on size. Taste a piece to test for doneness, or use a cake tester. Properly blanched vegetables are tender but firm enough to hold their shape. Remove the vegetables with the slotted spoon and transfer them to the ice bath. When they have cooled completely, drain them and proceed with the recipe. If you won't be using the blanched vegetables right away, transfer them to a dry container and refrigerate until using.

How to Make Tomato Sauce

Homemade tomato sauce is a breeze to make. I like to cook a big batch of sauce and then divide it into small containers and freeze it. Sauce will also last for a few days in the refrigerator. Tomatoes do tend to burn when cooked over high heat, so stir frequently. This particular sauce turns out best when using big, ripe red tomatoes, but canned tomatoes work as well. You also can add a few fresh oregano leaves.

Tomato Sauce   MAKES ABOUT 4 CUPS

2 pounds ripe tomatoes or two 28-ounce cans whole peeled tomatoes and their juices
¼ cup extra-virgin olive oil
1 small Spanish onion, diced
4 cloves garlic, chopped
16 large basil leaves
Kosher salt and freshly ground black pepper

If you are using fresh tomatoes, core the tomatoes, then chop them into large pieces and reserve any juices that collect on the cutting board. If you are using canned tomatoes, roughly chop them. In a large saucepan, heat the olive oil over medium heat and sauté the onion until it begins to color, 2 to 3 minutes. Add the garlic and sauté until lightly colored and fragrant, about 1 minute, then add the tomatoes and their juices. Bring to a simmer over medium-high heat, then reduce the heat to low and cook for 30 minutes for fresh tomatoes and 15 minutes for canned. Tear the basil leaves into pieces and add them to the sauce. Simmer for 5 additional minutes, then remove from the heat. Season with salt and pepper to taste. Let cool slightly. Using an immersion blender or a countertop blender, puree the sauce until smooth.

How to Cook Eggs

Eggs are magic. They're versatile and hold a place of honor in many cuisines. Eggs are an essential ingredient in everything from pasta to cakes and sauces and more. And there are few things better than creamy scrambled eggs over toast or a fried egg with a runny yolk to top a rice bowl.

Equipment

A good nonstick sauté pan with a lid is essential for cooking eggs. You'll also want a saucepan with a lid for poaching and boiling and a stiff silicone spatula for scrambling or frying.

Doneness

Eggs require a delicate touch. I like scrambled eggs soft and the yolks of poached and fried eggs runny. If you prefer them to be cooked a little more, just add time. Do not increase the heat under the pan when frying eggs, as that will only cook the outer edges of the egg faster. You want to cook fried eggs slowly and evenly. Cook scrambled eggs over medium heat. For poached eggs, use a gentle simmer.

Scrambled Eggs SERVES 2

4 large eggs
¼ cup half-and-half or whole milk
1 teaspoon kosher salt
2 tablespoons unsalted butter
3 tablespoons crème fraîche or sour cream
¼ teaspoon freshly ground black pepper

In a bowl, vigorously whisk the eggs with the half-and-half. Add the salt. In a nonstick sauté pan, melt the butter over medium heat until it begins to bubble. Pour the eggs into the pan and use a stiff silicone spatula to spin the eggs in a circular motion, scraping the sides to make sure the eggs don't stick. Continue doing this until the eggs begin to set and turn opaque. Add the crème fraîche and continue cooking until the eggs are cooked through but still soft. Sprinkle on the pepper and serve.

Optional: When adding the crème fraîche, you could also add a handful of grated cheddar or 2 tablespoons grated Parmesan.

Poached Eggs MAKES 2 EGGS

If making a recipe with poached eggs, this will be the last step. Be sure to have all of your equipment and ingredients prepped before you start cooking.

2 tablespoons distilled vinegar
2 large eggs
Kosher salt and freshly ground black pepper

In a medium saucepan, bring 2 quarts room temperature water and the vinegar to a boil. Reduce the heat until just simmering. Carefully crack one egg into a small bowl and gently slip it into the water. Repeat with the other egg. Make sure there is space between the eggs. Leave them undisturbed for 3 minutes. Use a slotted spoon to lift the eggs out of the water one at a time and drain on a paper towel–lined plate. Season with salt and pepper and serve immediately.

Hard-Boiled Eggs MAKES 4 EGGS

4 large eggs, room temperature

Prepare an ice bath as on page 225. Place the eggs in a medium saucepan and add water to cover by at least 2 inches. Bring the water to a boil, then reduce the heat until just simmering. Simmer for 6 minutes. Cover and remove from the heat. Let sit, covered, for 10 minutes. Pour the hot water from the pan and transfer the eggs to the ice bath. Allow to cool for 15 minutes. Gently peel the eggs. Hard-boiled eggs can be stored in the refrigerator for up to 4 days.

Fried Eggs MAKES 2 EGGS

1 tablespoon unsalted butter
2 large eggs
Kosher salt and freshly ground black pepper

For sunny-side up eggs, in a nonstick sauté pan, melt the butter over medium heat until it begins to bubble. Crack the eggs into the pan and let sit undisturbed until the whites begin to turn opaque. Add 2 teaspoons room temperature water, cover the pan with a lid, and reduce the heat to medium-low. Cook until the whites are completely set around the yolks; the yolks should still be bright yellow and uncooked. Slide the eggs onto a plate and season with salt and pepper.

For over-easy eggs, the idea is to flip your eggs and cook them to your desired doneness on both sides. Follow the steps above until the yolks are starting to cook. To flip the eggs, use a turner and carefully flip them one by one, being careful not to break the yolks. You can use the lid to turn the eggs: Remove it from the pan. Holding the pan at an angle, slide the eggs onto the inverted lid. Invert the pan and place it onto the lid upside down. Then, quickly turn the lidded pan right-side up so the eggs fall back into the pan. You may want to do this over the sink. Continue cooking over medium-low heat until the egg yolks are set and cooked to the desired doneness. Season with salt and pepper.

How to Cook Beans and Other Legumes

There is a whole world of dried beans and legumes, each with its own flavor to explore. In this book, I stick to varieties that are easy to find, but don't be afraid to try something new. I generally use water to cook beans and legumes, but you can try different stocks or add flavorings to up your bean game.

Although I prefer to cook beans and legumes myself, there's no shame in reaching for canned beans when you're short on time. My wife loves chickpeas in her lunchtime salads and they can be used straight from a can after a quick rinse. Canned beans are also good for a last-minute breakfast—pair them with eggs, a warm tortilla, and some sour cream and you're all set.

That said, it's not complicated to cook beans and most are forgiving. I prefer to soak beans in advance, but soaking isn't completely necessary—it simply saves a little time when cooking. Before cooking, spread the dried beans on a platter or baking sheet to look for and discard any foreign objects like small pebbles. After sorting through them, transfer them to a strainer and rinse them under cold water. From there, place the beans in a bowl, add cold water to cover by several inches (the beans will expand as they soak), cover the bowl, and set aside to soak for 1 to 2 hours. Alternatively, proceed with cooking without soaking.

To cook, place the beans in a large saucepan or stockpot. For 1 pound (about 3 cups) dried beans, add cold water to cover by a few inches and 1 tablespoon kosher salt. Add 1 small, peeled, whole Spanish onion. In a coffee filter, wrap 1 tablespoon black peppercorns, 1 to 2 sprigs thyme, and a few peeled garlic cloves. Tie the filter tightly with kitchen twine and add to the bean pot. Bring it all to a simmer and cook until the beans are tender. The cooking time will vary depending on the size and age of the beans, so check them frequently once they begin to soften. Let the beans cool in the cooking liquid; discard the coffee filter. Store the beans in their liquid in an airtight container in the refrigerator until ready to use or for up to 1 week.

Cooked Chickpeas

To cook chickpeas, rinse 1 pound (16 ounces) of dried chickpeas under cold water, then place in a bowl and cover with water and allow to soak for at least 2 hours. Drain and transfer the chickpeas to a large saucepan. Cover the chickpeas by about 3 inches with water, adding 1 teaspoon of salt for every 1 cup of water. Bring to a boil over high heat, then reduce the heat to a simmer. Simmer until they are tender but not falling apart, about 40 minutes. Drain and spread the chickpeas on a baking sheet or tray and allow to cool. You can also add 1 tablespoon of turmeric or ½ teaspoon cumin or coriander to 1 pound of chickpeas before bringing to a boil to add flavor and brighten the color.

Cooked Lentils

Lentils cook more quickly than beans. I love lentils, especially French or du puy lentils, as well as red lentils. Each variety has its own cooking time. Remember, you can always cook them longer but once they are overcooked you can't undo it, so keep an eye on them.

For every 1 cup of dried lentils I use 1 small Spanish onion, minced, and 1 teaspoon kosher salt. Sauté the onion in about 2 tablespoons of extra-virgin olive oil and add the lentils. Add vegetable stock to cover by about 2 inches and season with salt. Simmer until tender. Once the lentils are cooked, let them cool in the liquid.

Simple Black Beans MAKES ABOUT 3 CUPS

3 tablespoons canola oil

1 small Spanish onion, minced

3 cloves garlic, minced

2 cups cooked black beans

1 cup bean cooking liquid

1 Roasted Red Pepper (page 224), cut into small dice

1 small beefsteak tomato, cored and diced, juices reserved

2 teaspoons sherry vinegar

Kosher salt and freshly ground black pepper

In a large sauté pan, heat the canola oil over medium heat and add the onion and garlic. Sauté until they begin to color lightly. Add the cooked beans, cooking liquid, roasted pepper, and tomato. Bring to a simmer and cook for 10 minutes. Remove from the heat and stir in the vinegar. Season with salt and pepper. Transfer 1 cup of the bean mixture to a blender and puree until smooth. Fold the puree back into the beans. Serve hot.

How to Cook Pasta

Use a large pot that holds enough water to fully cover the pasta by several inches. To season the water with salt, use a ratio of about 1 tablespoon of kosher salt per 1 quart of water. Make sure the water comes to a rolling boil before adding the pasta. Once the pasta is added, give it a good stir to make sure nothing is sticking to the bottom of the pot.

For dried pasta, use the cooking times provided on the packaging as a guide. If you will be adding the cooked pasta to a sauce and cooking the two together on the stovetop, reduce the pasta cooking time by 1 to 2 minutes. Fresh pasta takes much less time to cook than dried pasta. The best way to test the doneness of pasta is by pulling out a piece and taking a bite. It should be tender but slightly firm in texture.

Acknowledgments

Having done this cookbook thing a few times now, I've become more and more respectful of the process and fully appreciate that making a book is a team sport. As in most things in life, you are only as good as the people around you; it's never about the individual. I feel as lucky as a person can be since both in and outside of work, I am surrounded by the best people in my friends, family, colleagues, and community.

I'm never sure where to start but my thanks go to: Michael Harlan Turkell for doing this with me a third time. Catrine Kelty for making the food look stunningly beautiful. George Restrepo and Lisa Diercks at Endpaper Studio for making everything jump off the page. Sandy Gilbert and the team at Rizzoli for bringing another dream of mine to life. Ryan Boyd and Christian Canevari from Row 34 for helping to pull the frantic photo shoots together. Kelsey Whitsett for the last-minute testing. And special thanks to Allyson Boyd for helping with the cookbook from start to finish—this wouldn't have happened without her.

Erin! It's our third adventure pulling a book together. Thank you for everything and mostly your patience when waiting for me to write. A lot has happened in our lives since we started doing this together, and I'm always grateful for your friendship and collaboration. You make it fun and easy.

To my business partner and friend Shore Gregory and his incredible wife, Celina, thanks for the never-ending support and for always making it fun. Also, a huge thanks to my amazing restaurant staffers who are relentless in their efforts to make each of the Row 34 restaurants so great.

Lastly, and most importantly, to my family: Lisa, Hudson, Ethan, and Sophia. You guys are my everything and will always be my favorite people to cook for.

—Jeremy Sewall

Diving into our third cookbook project together, I was impressed with just how quickly this team got into the groove. From recipe writing to chapter writing to headnotes to testing to photo shoots, the process went about as smoothly as these things can go. Just like a good recipe, once you've done it a few times, both the process and the end result become that much more enjoyable.

Jeremy! Thank you for sharing your projects with me and allowing me to come along for the ride. Not all chefs can just jot down a recipe that makes sense—you've become a pro at it, which makes my job a joy every time. I say it with each book but it's true: Your recipes make me want to cook. And because this one is all about home cooking, I'll also say thanks for creating a book just for me!

A double thanks to our team: Michael, Catrine, Ally, Sandy, George, Lisa, and the many other helpers along the way—your work has guided and improved this project at every turn.

My family did a fair amount of recipe sampling in support of this book—thank you to Dave, Charlie, and Maggie for being excellent kitchen helpers, dish washers, eaters, and cheerleaders. You guys make life more delicious.

—Erin Byers Murray

Index

(Page references in *italics* refer to illustrations.)

T

V

W

Y

Z

First published in the United States of America in 2025 by
Rizzoli International Publications, Inc.
49 West 27th Street
New York, NY 10001
www.rizzoliusa.com

Text copyright © 2025 Erin Byers Murray and Jeremy Sewall
Recipes copyright © 2025 Jeremy Sewall
Photography copyright © 2025 Michael Harlan Turkell with the exception of bottom of page 233 Mayter Scott
Publisher: Charles Miers
Project Editor: Sandra Gilbert Freidus
Design: Endpaper Studio
Production Manager: Rebecca Ambrose
Managing Editor: Lynn Scrabis
Food Styling: Catrine Kelty
Editorial Assistance: Natalie Danford, Tricia Levi
Indexer: Cathy Dorsey

Library of Congress Control Number: 2025935956

MIX
Paper | Supporting responsible forestry
FSC™ C007683

Printed in China
2025 2026 2027 2028 / 10 9 8 7 6 5 4 3 2 1
ISBN: 978-0-8478-7430-9
The authorized representative in the EU for product safety and compliance is Mondadori Libri S.p.A., via Gian Battista Vico 42, Milan, Italy, 20123.
www.mondadori.it

Visit us online:
Facebook.com/RizzoliNewYork
Instagram.com/rizzolibooks
Youtube.com/user/RizzoliNY